PATHWAYS TO DESTINY

Life from Conception to Fulfillment

By
Taiwo Ogbomo

Contents

Appreciation vii
Introduction. ix
1   What Is Destiny. 15
2   Framework of Destiny 24
3   Levels of Destiny Operations 33
4   Free Will 47
5   Resources 53
6   Times and Seasons 64
7   Revelation. 78
8   Divine Appointment 90
9   The Journey to Destiny .106
10   Clues from the Past. 121
11   God and People Focused. 133
12   Destiny Busters. 147
13   Staying On Course 158

Appreciation

T he substance of a message, and the evolving identity of a messenger, is derived from the sender. I am most grateful to God Almighty for His great love and faithfulness toward me.

I appreciate the privilege and inspiration to commence and complete this book that promises to help people fulfill their God-premeditated destinies. In You I live and move and have my being.

I wish to express my profound gratitude to Dr. Solomon Babajide for taking time to extensively review this book and for providing the benefit of his vast wisdom and experience.

To my lovely wife, partner, helper, and friend for her unconditional love and support of my endeavors, including the pursuit of my calling. Thank you for your compassion, wise counsel, and sacrifices over the years and for listening to God when He speaks. You are indeed a precious gift from God to me, and I will forever love you.

To Osamede, Etinosa, and Abiuwa, the best children a father can hope for; thank you for cheering me on and for your understanding and support as I take time out in temporary solitude to focus on work. I love you.

Introduction

"There is not a spider hanging on the king's wall that does not have its errand; there is not a nettle that grows in the corner of the churchyard that does not have its purpose; there is not a single insect fluttering in the breeze that does not accomplish some divine decree; and I will never have it that God created any man, especially any Christian man, to be a blank and to be a nothing. He made you for an end. Find out what that end is. Find out your niche and fill it. If it is ever so little, if it is only to be a chopper of wood and a drawer of water, do something in this great battle for God and truth."
– Charles Haddon Spurgeon

P eople often ponder the questions: What will my life become? What am I here on earth to accomplish? What should I do to be the person God created me to be? What does my future hold? And ultimately this: What is my destiny? Attempts to satisfy this yearning often drive people to things, places, and persons that in many cases further complicate their search for answers.

In my teenage years I often pondered what my destiny would be. I had no clue what the future held for me or how events in my life would unfold. Consequently I went on a search to unravel the puzzle of life, particularly as it pertains to the question of destiny. I read as many books and articles as I could lay my hands on but could not find compelling answers. At age eighteen I came across what I thought was the closest answer—an article that suggested destiny is being in the right place at the right time. I had an "aha" moment and thought this was profound as the timing coincided with a period in which I was preparing to relocate to the United States. I thought this must surely be it. *Now*, I said to myself, *I am heading to the right place (the most coveted country in the world) at the right time.*

One problem was that the United States is a huge country with fifty states. Then came more questions: Which of these states is the right place? Which city should I settle in? Where should I attend college? What should I study? These and many other questions flooded my mind all over again. I began to realize that destiny is much more than *being in the right place at the right time*.

In this book we will look at the function of time and location in the pathways to destiny, as well as many other crucial concepts that will serve as useful guides as we navigate through the pathways to fulfilling our destinies.

Destiny is discovered when hidden dreams, talents, and aspirations find outlets for expression. It is being where you ought to be and doing what you are best suited to do in order to optimize your potential in life. Destiny is often incorrectly used interchangeably with "fate" or "fortune." Fate and fortune are different in that they pertain to predetermined and unavoidable courses of events and outcomes irrespective of where you are and the decisions you make. The concept of fate and fortune is based on the belief that one's life is anchored to the fixed natural order of the cosmos, to events that are inevitable.

Destiny entails a convergence of multiple interrelated life paths in a lifelong journey. Life isn't one straight path but consists of multiple paths with twists and turns as you will discover. Destiny as a term is often misunderstood. I can appreciate the ambiguity surrounding this term and its usage. A reference to different dictionaries may further complicate your understanding as there are various uses and meanings floating around. One dictionary defines destiny as "something that is to happen or has happened to a particular person or thing; lot or fortune." This suggests that a person has no role to play in the outcome of their lives. Another definition is "the predetermined, usually inevitable or irresistible, course of events." Yet another definition of destiny is "the power or agency that determines the course of events." This is somewhat interesting as it is the force or being that determines the course of events. This notion suggests that the outcome of a person's life is orchestrated by some unnamed force or being that pulls the strings, and a person has no control or influence over the outcome of their life.

Is one's life determined by an event or combination of events? Is one's destiny inevitable, or can it be thwarted? Is the outcome of a person's life solely dependent on some external force or forces, or does the person have a role to play and free will to exercise? We will address these and other questions in our journey together as we explore the *Pathways to Destiny*.

Inasmuch as there are differing viewpoints on what destiny is, it only makes sense to turn to God, the Creator, to discover what it is. Destiny is actually a God concept and should be seen from His viewpoint. When we want to learn about a product, we look to its manufacturer. A product manufacturer (such as car, machinery, or equipment) has a specific purpose for its products and conditions under which they provide the most utility. So it is with destiny. Destiny and purpose go hand-in-hand. It is important to know our collective purpose here on earth as God's creations. It is equally necessary to live out and fulfill our individually distinct mandates. Each one of us has distinct roles and specific missions that God has predetermined for us to fulfill here on earth.

People often make the mistake of comparing themselves to others. When comparisons are made, inaccurate criteria are used to track progress toward the fulfillment of one's destiny, and then destinies are misguided and thwarted. Comparisons can distort one's judgment and lead people to covetousness and misperception of God as biased, whereas everyone's destiny is special to God. God does not assess the outcome of our lives by measuring our accomplishments through a universal yardstick, but rather by our ability to deliver results consistent with the responsibilities, gifts, and talents He has given us.

Consider the parable of the talents in Matthew 25:14-30, in which the master disbursed varying amounts of talents to his servants. Neither the amount of talent received nor the amount they had in their possession when the master returned were as important as the servants' faithfulness in stewarding the talents they received. If you received one talent but became preoccupied and discontent with the fact that another person received five, you stand the danger of not fulfilling your utmost potential with the one talent that was handed to you. This is a major reason why many do not fulfill their destiny—comparing themselves with others.

Many people like to travel in packs and desire the same accomplishments, occupations, and lifestyles as others. Consequently, they find it difficult to see their unique capabilities and to harness their

God-given uniqueness to accomplish their individual mandates and fulfill their destinies. Hence the vast majority of people die never fulfilling their destinies.

I was in a theology classroom when someone raised a question about predestination. As we discussed whether God is fair in allowing some people to be born into wealth while others are born into poverty, the discussion got quite complex with no answers. We concluded that people do not have a say in what geographical location they are brought up in, which families they are born into, the times in which they live (whether of peace or war), and so forth.

At the end of our discussion we leaned on the side of fate and fortune since we could not find concrete answers for the disparities of conditions in which people find themselves. Our position had an underlying assumption that someone born poor, or in undesirable circumstances, is unlikely to compete effectively with his more fortunate counterpart. As a result of his disadvantage, he is not likely to optimize his potential on earth. Another flawed assumption is that the outcomes of our lives are measured by some universal yardstick that involves wealth, possession, power, influence, and the things people put much premium on and are inclined to pursue.

Twelve hours after my classroom experience, while I was having my time of Bible study and meditation the next morning, I had a strong urge to write a book on destiny, and the Spirit of God began to pour answers into my spirit. I found myself reading through the book of Exodus with an understanding that was radically different from other times when I read the same narrative.

Over the next several months, as I read through different portions of the Bible, my understanding was reinforced and expanded as I was able to corroborate additional discoveries with inspired insights. As I observed the lives of the patriarchs in the Bible, and others who have left significant footprints on the sands of history, I came away with some amazing discoveries that will be of great help to you as you journey the paths of life toward fulfilling your destiny. Questions relating to destiny that are often raised but continue to elude easy answers are therefore the reasons for writing this book.

As you read I encourage you to take time to reflect on your own life, jot down your thoughts, do the exercises at the end of the chapters, and be intentional about piecing your own destiny puzzle together. Be courageous in correcting missteps and embracing your destiny pathways; and as you travel the pathways of your destiny expect fulfillment, joy, and satisfaction that money and possessions will not give you, as you make a lasting impact on the earth.

Chapter One:

What Is Destiny?

"For in Him we live and move and have our being, as also some of your own poets have said, 'For we are also His offspring.'"
– Acts 17:28

"You were born to make manifest the glory of God that is within you. It's not just in some of us; it's in everyone. And as you let your own light shine, you unconsciously give other people permission to do the same. As you are liberated from your own fear, your presence automatically liberates others."
– Nelson Mandela

Destiny is God's premeditated outcome for your life. It involves a lifelong journey with twists and turns—a life that emanates from God and ends with God. Destiny is the overall outcome of a person's life forged by cumulative experiences, events, choices, and decisions. We do not have control over some biographic factors surrounding our lives such as place of birth, era in which we exist, families to which we are born, and our innate gifts. Such factors are predetermined by God, the originator of life. Major events that occur throughout our lives may or may not be God's doing as a contrary force of evil works in opposition to God's perfect plan for us. The exercise of our free will plays a major role in the outcome of our lives. When our free will is exercised in alignment with God's purpose, everything falls into its proper place.

When God created man, He did so with a purpose – to exercise dominion and subdue the earth. Genesis 1:26-28 says: "Then God said, Let Us make man in Our image, according to Our likeness; let them have dominion over the fish of the sea, over the birds of the air, and over the cattle, over all the Earth and over every creeping thing that creeps on the Earth. So God created man in His own image; in the image of God He created him; male and female He created them. Then God blessed them, and God said to them, 'Be fruitful and multiply; fill the Earth and subdue it; have dominion over the fish of the sea, over the birds of the air, and over every living thing that moves on the Earth.'"

God never intended that we wander through life or leave the outcome of our lives to chance. God has deliberate purpose for mankind individually and collectively. Man was created to dominate and subdue in all areas of life on earth. This prerogative can be fully exercised by man under ideal circumstances in which both man and God are key players with ability to introduce variable inputs with deliberate outputs in mind. God has a desired (but not inevitable) outcome for everyone's life. Knowing what God's plan is and the choices you make will determine if the God-desired outcome is actualized. In order to gain a firm grasp on the concept of destiny so that you can be poised to fulfill yours, it helps to glean through the creation story of Adam and Eve.

In the pages that follow, you will discover some foundational dynamics that have the potential to help you through the rest of your life. In the creation narrative, you will notice three key elements: *decision, specification, and purpose*.

The Decision

Every creation, organism, invention, enterprise, and existence begins with a decision. The decision determines the life form and purpose of the creation. When a creation, invention, or enterprise lives out their purpose, they bring joy and fulfillment to their originator, and they are deemed successful, valued, and celebrated. However, when they fall short of their purpose and fail to fulfill the originator's intent, they breed discontent, lack of fulfillment, and leave a void to be filled. This is so even if they continue to exist somewhat and appear to provide alternative utility.

Similar to other forms of creation, invention, and enterprise, the creation of man began with a divine decision by the Godhead (Father, Son, and Holy Spirit). God, the originator, began with the decision to make man in His image and according to His likeness.

You are not an accident. You are far too special to be a result of some big-bang incident or evolution from some animal. Buildings, cars, technology, animals, and so forth do not just arbitrarily appear. Everything created in the beginning was created by God. God was very deliberate with His decision to create you, and He did not create you to stumble through life. He designed you with some very special outcome in mind. God is so interested in your success that He made you with unique qualities and attributes that closely resemble His own attributes and qualities. You were made in His image and likeness and have embedded within you peculiar attributes and specifications that can only be found in God.

The Specification

When the decision was made to create man, the specification was defined: *"Let us make man according to our likeness."* You need to understand God's nature, attributes, and capabilities in order to better understand yourself because He made you to be like Him. Following are some of the attributes, capabilities, and specifications that can help you better appreciate the inherent qualities within you:

Created to Shine as Light

Psalm 104:2a says that God covers Himself with light as with a garment. In John 1:8-9, Jesus is identified as "the true Light that gives light to every man coming to the world." He is the embodiment of light and gave light (lit up) to everyone coming to this world for the purpose of eradicating darkness from others on earth. In John 9:5 Jesus identifies Himself as "the Light of the world," which means that you are light in the world just like Him. In Matthew 5:14 Jesus Himself testifies that *"you are the light of the world. A city that is set on a hill cannot be hidden."* You were equipped with "light," metaphorically speaking, to be light like Jesus. Jesus did not carry a lamp around in His day but was compassionate and let His life be used by God to bless others as "He went about doing good" (Acts 10:38).

Jesus identified problems in His day and brought about solutions. Wherever you find yourself is the set place and platform where you can make a difference; act accordingly and make a difference. In Matthew 5:16 Jesus admonishes His followers to *"let your light so shine amongst all men."* Jesus is a genius. In the parable of the talents and in many of His teachings He indicated that your success, or destiny, is centered on your application of inherent gifts to add value to the lives of others.

Could you say that you are a light wherever you are momentarily? Does that light shine amongst people? If not, why not? When you acquire a fluorescent lamp or light bulb, for example, you determine where to place it for maximum utility. The light in front of your house serves a different purpose than the light inside your house. They both give light nonetheless. God intends for your light to be seen by others. God is the true light that gives light to you and determines your setting, or where you may shine. In the creation narrative (Genesis 1) we find that the earth was covered with darkness, but when God showed up He caused light (greater and lesser lights to appear) and determined where these lights are to shine.

Similarly, God created us and put us in different places where our light can shine and make a difference to our environment. The configuration of your light may be different from that of others, but certainly is not insignificant. Not being in the right place in conjunction with your light configuration can result in inability to fulfill destiny or optimize potential. For example, Jesus could not perform many miracles in Nazareth because of their unbelief (see Matthew 13:58). If Jesus' potential could be limited by His environment, so can yours. If you are in a place where your light (gifts, talents, abilities) is inhibited, then you need to be repositioned, as Jesus was. You were specially made to bring light to certain places and situations.

Created Glorious

You were made glorious. A distorted view of ourselves and low self-esteem often derail us from the purpose of God for our lives. Your thinking, self-perception, and self-assessment are tied to your destiny. However, while we are made in God's image and likeness, we should not attempt to partake in God's glory, which He has reserved exclusively for Himself. In 1 Peter 5:11, Galatians 1:5, and Philippians 4:20, the Bible makes it clear that "to God be glory and dominion forever and ever." Psalm 113:4 says that "God is above all, and His Glory above the heavens." In Job 40:10 God (in whose image we are made) describes Himself as being "adorned with majesty and splendor, and arrayed with glory and beauty." In

Psalm 26:8 David said, "Lord, I have loved the habitation of your house, and the place where your glory dwells."

There is a place where God's glory dwells, so by inference there is a place where your glory is to dwell and be revealed. You are celebrated in the place where your glory is made manifest. A weed is a plant in an unwanted place. A rosebush, irrespective of how beautiful it is, cannot prosper in a football field because it is in the wrong place. Similar to our light, we should seek to be where our gifts and talents are appreciated and allowed to blossom.

Psalm 8:4-5 (NASB) says, "What is man that You take thought of him, and the son of man that You care for him? Yet You have made him a little lower than God, and You crown him with glory and majesty!" God is so mindful of you that He crowned you with glory and majesty. Be careful to look beyond your closets and your physical needs and desires. In Matthew 6:28-30 Jesus taught His disciples not to worry and said that if God so clothed the grass of the field with more glory than King Solomon in all his physical glory, He will clothe as many as have faith in Him. In Psalm 3:3 David said, "But You, O Lord, are a shield for me, my glory and the One who lifts up my head." God created us glorious. If we have God as our glory, we can expect Him to lift up our heads.

Made Marvelous

You were made with extraordinary qualities. Moses expressed the awesomeness of God as he sang the song of victory at the Red Sea crossing. In Exodus 15:11 he exclaimed, "Who is like You, O Lord, among the gods? Who is like You, glorious in holiness, fearful in praises, doing wonders?" What a true revelation of who God is! God gave a similar revelation to David a while later (Psalm 139:14) when he remarked about this God-like creation (man and woman), "I will praise You, for I am fearfully and wonderfully made."

Just as our Creator is fearful and wonderful, so are we. We are to be feared by spiritual forces and all creatures that God has given us dominion over on the earth, in heavenly places, in the sea, and beneath the earth and sea. We are to be feared by opposition forces that try to undermine our destiny. And it is God's design that signs and wonders should follow us (Isaiah 8:18, Mark 16:17-20, Hebrews 2:4). Unfortunately for those that do not know who they are in Christ, Satan will attempt to intimidate them and place them under his control so that they do not fulfill their destiny.

When Moses' glory was revealed, he was as a god to the Israelites, to whom he was called, and to Pharaoh, their oppressor and taskmaster (see Exodus 4:16, 7:1). When God exalted Joshua, the people submitted to him (Joshua chapters 3-24). So it was with Gideon, who was marginalized until God raised him to be a judge. Thereafter, his people and their oppressor feared Gideon (see Judges 6-7).

Made Powerful

God is powerful and created us to be powerful. Everyone that believes in the Lord has the privilege of receiving the promised Holy Spirit (Acts 1:8). In John 1:12 we are told that "as many as received Him, to them He gave power to become children of God." If you have received Christ, you are redeemed and powerful. You are empowered "to trample on serpents, scorpions and over all the power of the enemy and nothing can hurt you" (Luke 10:19). You are so empowered that "whatever you bind on earth has been bound in heaven, and whatever you loose on earth has been loosed in heaven" (Matthew 18:18). This is very much like God, who declares a thing and behold it is done! This privilege is available only to those reconciled by the work of redemption to our heavenly Father through His Son, Jesus Christ. For those devoid of this heritage as God's son or daughter, there is no power. The power of the believer is not set to autopilot. You must utilize the power God gives you for the fulfillment of your destiny.

Endowed with Creative Abilities

God made us with creative abilities. Consider the creation of the universe, the various ways God delivered victory in times of trouble and war to our patriarchs, and the diverse methods Jesus used to heal the sick. Also consider our advancement in science, technology, and other areas – all because we have God's creative nature. God replenished a depleted earth and redeemed mankind from the fall in the Garden of Eden. God made us with innate creative abilities that must be utilized.

In order to optimize our creative potentials we need the Holy Spirit. We are told in 1 Corinthians 2:9 that "Eyes have not seen, ears have not heard, nor have entered into the heart of men what God has for those who love Him, but they are revealed by the Holy Spirit." Revelation, often termed "discovery," is an important aspect of creativity. We will discuss revelation in more detail later in this book.

Purpose

God made us for His purpose. You are not an accident as big-bang theorists would like you to believe. Instead, we were created for a purpose that entails that we exercise dominion. God never intended for us to live like wanderers, in defeat, or as slaves on earth. He made us and sent us here on a mission and equipped us with light to dispel darkness from a dark world—empowered to exercise dominion over every creature (physical and spiritual). We were created to exercise authority and dominion, to be full of might, to be fruitful, to reproduce after our kind, to be problem solvers and the light of the world. These and other qualities of God can manifest themselves in our lives in varying forms and degrees. The path to fulfilling our destiny begins with knowing why we were made.

The disconnect

Since our origin is from God, and we were created to exercise dominion on earth, you may wonder why the vast majority of people do not live lives of dominion or come short of fulfilling their destinies. Why is there so much pain in the world? Why are there so many hurting people out there seeking solutions to no avail? Why isn't a person's destiny apparent? And so forth.

I will present two key reasons pertaining to *identity* and *displacement*. Romans 3:23 says that "all have sinned and fall short of the glory of God."

Identity: The vast majority of people that walk through life lack proper understanding of who they are. If you do not know who you are, what your purpose on earth is, and the resources at your disposal to accomplish your mission, you will not get clear direction and consequently will not fulfill your destiny. This explains why accumulation of wealth and material things does not satisfy the yearning within, when someone is not living in harmony with their God-predetermined purpose. Unfortunately, many live and subsequently die never finding their purpose and fulfillment. You need to know who you are, what your purpose is, and the resources that are available to you.

The call of God on the prophet Jeremiah provides us with great insight into how identity and displacement work. Prior to receiving revelation, Jeremiah did not know God's predetermined purpose for his life. In Jeremiah 1 we see how the prophet thought of himself as inadequate and unable to fulfill his God-ordained destiny: "Ah, Lord God! behold, I cannot speak: for I am a child." He could not see that there was a *decision* backed with intent (*purpose*) and capabilities (*specifications*) provided to enable him to accomplish his destiny.

If Jeremiah had continued to lack knowledge of his purpose and God-given capabilities, and continued to consign himself to a place of incapability (displaced and immature) he would never have fulfilled his destiny. When Jeremiah felt inadequate, God was there to help him discover and identify those capabilities (specifications) needed to fulfill his destiny. Jeremiah's purpose was connected to the specific place and people to which he was called.

Displacement: When Adam and Eve sinned against God, they were displaced from the Garden of Eden where they were meant to exercise dominion. Through Adam, we all were born into sin and are consequently displaced from our rightful place of dominion. Romans 3:23 says "all have sinned and fall short of the glory of God." The sin that came to humanity through Adam/Eve separated everyone from God and consequently caused the loss of privileges (Isaiah 59:2). Adam/Eve were wrapped in the glory of God and put in the Garden of Eden where they were meant to exercise dominion and manifest their God-given glory.

It is important that you know who you are as a child of God made in His image and likeness, with all the attributes, qualities, characteristics, and capabilities of God. Lions give birth to lions, and goats give birth to goats. The Word says: "But as many as received Him, to them He gave the right to become children of God, to those who believe in His name: who were born, not of blood, nor of the will of the flesh, nor of the will of man, but of God" (John 1:12-13). You are God's child, created in God's image to resemble Him. "You are gods, and all of you are children of the Most High" (Psalm 82:6-7).

God created us to exercise dominion and subdue the earth, which would require us to be fruitful, multiply, and fill the earth as Adam and Eve were commanded. In His sovereign power, God blessed and empowered them to accomplish this purpose. If God stopped there, we would leave all the responsibility of fulfilling our destinies to God. But He didn't. He gave humankind free will, which is addressed at great length in chapter four of this book. God is the originator of life. In order to understand your purpose and what your destiny holds, you must find your identity and purpose in God, "for in Him we live and move and have our being, as also some of your own poets have said, 'For we are also His offspring'" (Acts 17:28).

What is destiny therefore? Destiny is God's premeditated outcome for your life, which entails knowing your unique *specification,* as well as discovering and living out your preordained *purpose* on earth. It is identifying what you are here for and being intentional in your efforts to fulfill God's plan for your life.

Chapter questions:
1. Have you been born-again – reconciled back to God by accepting His Son Jesus Christ?

2. In what areas do you feel inadequate or handicapped, like Prophet Jeremiah? Pray for God's perspective.

3. How are you uniquely wired to make a difference in the world?

4. What God-like attributes can you bring to bear in the world starting today?
    a. Are you properly positioned to shine?
    b. Where is the ideal place for your unique attributes to flourish? If you aren't there what is stopping you?

Chapter Two:

Framework of Destiny

"…O Lord, you are our Father. We are the clay, and You are our potter. And all we are the work of Your hand."
– Isaiah 64:8

"We are not creatures of circumstance; we are creators of circumstance."
– Benjamin Disraeli

Our destiny begins and ends with God. God has a framework in which our destiny is discovered and fulfilled. Within God's framework, He has given us freedom to make choices that either keep us in the path to fulfillment or derail us from our destiny. For freedom of choice and decisions to work in our advantage, we must recognize the boundaries God put in place and exercise our choices within those parameters. God is the potter and we are the clay. We are the handiwork of God, the Creator of everything. He created us; we did not create ourselves. As clay we cannot determine the form we will take or the outcome of our lives. God had a predetermined outcome in mind before embarking on the project of creation, just as a potter would have a vision of the outcome of his pottery, or an architect would have an image in mind of an architectural design before embarking on a project.

You can take comfort in knowing that in God's goodness, He has your best interests at heart. Just as you would expect a talented artist such as Rembrandt, Picasso, Da Vinci, and Van Gogh, with their inherent shortcomings, to develop exceptional artwork, you expect a flawless God to make the best of your life as you completely yield to Him. God remains the awesome Creator of the heavens, the earth, and all the wonders contained therein that we are yet to wrap our arms around. To imagine God's creative abilities, think about our galaxy and all its phenomenal wonders and intricacies. In spite of technological advancement and the discoveries we have had, there is a wealth of discovery yet to be made. We still have a long way to go to unravel God's abundant and complex creations.

The human body is the most complex machine man has ever known. God said to Jeremiah, "Before I formed you in the womb I knew you; before you were born I sanctified you; I ordained you a prophet to the nations" (Jeremiah 1:5). God created Jeremiah for a specific purpose: to be a prophet to the nations. He also created you for a specific purpose. You have a specific mission to accomplish. Knowing your purpose and working to fulfill it can be exhilarating and refreshing. Deviation from God's purpose will lead to frustration, whereas submission and exercise of our free will in line with God's plan and purpose will always produce the desired result – the fulfillment of our destiny.

Divine Invitation

Divine purpose and calling is not peculiar to Jeremiah. We are all called to specific purposes. The Bible says that "all things work together for good to those who love God, to those who are the called according to His purpose. For whom He foreknew, He also predestined to be conformed to the image of His Son, that He might be the firstborn among many brethren. Moreover whom He predestined, these He also called; whom He called, these He also justified; and whom He justified, these He also glorified" (Romans 8:28-30).

God created us for and is calling each of us to something great, where He will have us "glorified," but we need to discover what His calling is in our lives. Success in life can be defined as the ability to harness innate gifts and talents in order to fulfill one's purpose and calling. It is never too late to begin utilizing our gifts toward fulfilling our destiny. What is important is to yield to the call of God now and in the future, as His calling evolves with times and seasons.

It should be understood that God reveals our calling when we are of age and perhaps when we have the discipline for the mission. In the meantime, He uses the experiences of life to prepare us for what is to come. God is patient and will not give you responsibilities He knows you cannot handle. Often He will wait for you to develop the experiences and maturity, as well as the capacity to handle the responsibilities He has for you. Or He might orchestrate the appropriate experience and situation to prepare you. Either way, God will take you to your next step in the journey to fulfilling your destiny when you have met the prerequisites for that step and yielded yourself to His desired workings. He will bring you along to the next phase in life's journey when the preparatory objectives of the present phase have been met. Put another way, you get promoted to the next level when you have demonstrated adequate preparation.

When God called Abram he was asked to "get out of [his] country, from [his] family and from [his] father's house, to a land that [God] will show [him]" (Genesis 12:1). Abram, in his human consideration, as many today would, took his father and nephew along. He did not get very far in that journey. After the death of his father, Tehrah, Abram still had his nephew, Lot, with him and struggled in his journey to destiny. And even when he came to the Promised Land, he went past it because he wasn't quite ready for the next phase (Genesis 12:5-7). Abram could not settle in God's preferred destination for his life until he was separated from Lot, who represented a class of people (his father's house) that God asked him to get out from. This underscores the need to yield completely to God on the way to destiny.

Maturity enables us to make informed, though sometimes difficult, decisions. It makes it easier to discern relationships and habits that are counterproductive in our bid to fulfill destiny, and to avoid them. We must bear in mind that even though God calls us, in His gentle nature He will never compel us against our will. God's calling upon our life is an invitation to embrace His plan and purpose for our lives. If you choose to yield to God's plan, you will have a winning blueprint for a successful life, irrespective of how uncertain things may sometimes appear. Should you decide on a path different from God's plan for your life, it is only reasonable to expect either to not find fulfillment or not arrive at your destiny at all.

When God calls, in the exercise of your freedom of choice, you can decide to say yes or no; agree or disagree; listen and obey, or tune out and disobey. The choice is yours. If you are listening,

God is always speaking. We sometimes fail to hear God because we allow noises around us to hinder our ability to hear Him, who often speaks in a still small voice (see 1 Kings 19:12). We also tend to keep ourselves busy and pretend not to hear or understand what God is saying, in an act of disobedience or immaturity, as toddlers do when they pretend not to understand basic instructions.

Although God does not compel us against our will, there are compelling consequences to the choices we make. No one is exempt from the consequences of poor choices. Not even Moses was exempt. In Exodus 4:24 we see that Moses was about to be killed by God for his disobedience and failure to circumcise his son. If Zipporah had not stepped in to perform God's requirement, Moses would have died and God would have raised up another "deliverer" to continue His corporate plan for Israel.

God speaks all the time: He speaks to us when we read the Bible, His Word. He speaks through genuine prophets or teachers of God's Word. He speaks through dreams and through the advice of elders and people with godly wisdom. He speaks in diverse ways. God's words are often subtle but occasionally loud. They are sometimes direct and at other times indirect. Irrespective of what God says and how He says it, heeding the voice of God brings us closer to our destiny. Ignoring or disobeying His voice will cause us to drift from our destiny or remain unnecessarily stagnant.

God calls us according to His purpose, not ours. He does not call us in areas that seem preferable to us but to Him. Though you may have other pursuits at the time of God's calling, He often calls you to a purpose for which He has given you a level of interest and passion. When God called Moses, it was in an area in which God had already given him interest (see Exodus 2:11-13). Before Paul was called to be an apostle of the faith, he was very religious and well-versed in Judaism but resisted the Christian faith because he did not have revelation of the truth. God used the same zeal and passion Paul had in his bid to enforce Judaic laws to advance the Christian faith after his conversion (Gala*tians 1:13-16*).

We do not all respond to the needs and issues in our communities the same way. We have proclivities and gravitate more toward certain issues than others. We need to pay attention to our innate gifts, interests, and passions, as they are often pointers to our destiny. The Bible says that "a man's gift makes room for him, and brings him before great men" (Proverbs 18:16). Appropriately applying your gifts and talents could help further the realization of your destiny. When selfish motives and immediate gains are not the driving factors, your interests, passions, and talents make a way for you, and material blessings follow. It is critical to know that material blessings often follow the pursuit of God-given passions and interests.

David was not inspired by selfish motives when he took on the Goliath challenge. However, he did well to recognize, confirm, and receive the benefits promised to anyone who defeated Goliath (1 Samuel 17:25-27). If the material incentives were absent, there is every indication that David would nevertheless have confronted Goliath. Rather than living for the material things of this world, as most people do, Jesus said that you should "seek first the kingdom of God and His righteousness, and all these things shall be added to you" (Matthew 6:33). The desire to advance God's kingdom should never be for personal gain but out of genuine interest and passion to be a part of what God is doing.

As you consider God's calling upon your life, rest assured that He will provide everything you need to succeed. Jesus asked the disciples to "follow me, and I will make you become fishers of men" (Mark 1:17). God has all it takes to make you into what He has called you to be. Like a solvent employer, God provides the tools, information, and resources you need to accomplish all that He has for you. He also justifies and endorses you. You may not realize the greater extent of your capabilities, but God does. Moses did not recognize his potentials and capabilities when God called him. He was afraid that his fellow Israelites and Pharaoh wouldn't listen to him. He had what he thought were human limitations (see Exodus 4-6). But those weren't barriers in the sight of God. With God's hand of justification and endorsement upon Moses' life, everyone listened, including Pharaoh.

When you heed God's calling upon your life, He justifies you and gives you a platform that enables you to execute His plans for your life. Having called and justified you, God glorifies you at the culmination of destiny. "Moreover whom He predestined, these He also called; whom He called, these He also justified; and whom He justified, these He also glorified" (Romans 8:30).

At the stage of glorification, God helps you get to the place of rest and fulfillment. The place of glorification may involve material blessings but goes beyond that. Moses is not portrayed in the Bible as one with accumulation of material wealth. We do not have a record of Moses possessing much gold, silver, land, and other precious metals or stones of his own. They were not necessary, as Moses had far more intangible assets and blessings that all began with Moses heeding the call of God. He brought the Israelites out of Egypt, and though he did not enter the Promised Land, he accomplished his calling, fulfilled his destiny, inherited glory, and left an eternal legacy behind.

To attain true greatness and glory, it is important that you take your eyes off the glamour and distractions of material rewards. Avoid getting stuck seeking rewards: cars, houses, money, positions, and so on. While there is nothing wrong with possessing these, there is much more than these to your life (see Matthew 6:25). Rewards and blessings should be embraced within the context of your calling. Life is ultimately about knowing your calling, embracing it, and fulfilling your destiny. Life is about knowing and fearing God (Exodus 19:5, Psalm 135:5, Ecclesiastes 12:13), knowing what He desires of you (Psalm 38:9, Lamentations 3:25), and in all humility obeying Him (John 9:31, James 4:10, 1 Peter 5:6).

In the pathways to your destiny, it is vital to recognize that while destiny is God's predetermined outcome for your life, life itself is a journey. The totality of life's journey, if completely yielded to God, culminates in God's predetermined destiny for you. A life lived outside of destiny is a life wasted.

About 320 years before Moses was born, God told Abraham that the Israelites would be in bondage and that He would bring them out after 400 years to the Promised Land. For the Israelites to come out of captivity in Egypt to Canaan, a series of events had to take place, some of which were orchestrated by God Almighty and others that fell within the control of the people. For example, God did not give Moses advance details of how He would afflict Pharaoh with ten plagues, nor did He provide Moses with a detailed roadmap and exit strategy for the exodus. He did, however, tell Moses that He would "harden Pharaoh's heart" (Exodus 7:3). Within this framework, God informed Moses that his responsibility was to go to Pharaoh as He led. God would orchestrate things, including the hardening of

Pharaoh's heart, in the course of bringing the Israelites out of bondage. Moses was wise to follow God's prompting and instructions, plague after plague.

Anyone who wants to fulfill his God-ordained destiny has the crucial responsibility to follow God's lead in complete obedience through his life's journey and not give up prematurely when faced with challenges along the way. If you make the right choices, in line with God's will for your life, you will get to your destination. After nine plagues, "the LORD said to Moses, 'I will bring one more plague on Pharaoh and on Egypt. Afterward he will let you go from here. When he lets you go, he will surely drive you out of here altogether'" (Exodus 11:1). At this juncture, a question remained pertaining to where the Israelites were going upon departure from their comfort zone in Egypt. Where precisely were they going, from this place of certainty to uncertainty? That is the sort of question many people ask either directly or indirectly. It comes up repeatedly when making major decisions in life.

A prospective entrepreneur, for example, may wonder which venture to pursue amongst multiple options and what path he should take. When choosing a career path, one may wonder which path will bring about fulfillment in life. When making major life decisions, the starting point could be daunting because of the uncertainty of the future and unknown variables. However, we can proceed with confidence knowing that if God is the One leading, we can trust Him to bring us to our destination because He possesses complete knowledge and absolute power.

Faith

As with Moses, God made a promise to Abraham about what He planned to do through him, but He did not provide a detailed map or complete picture of the path to fulfillment. Neither Moses nor Abraham had been through their God-ordained experiences before, which further cast doubts on their ability to reach their destinations. So it is with you. It is not too common for God to show the end from the beginning – even though He knows it very well. There is much you will not know, and not knowing all the details of how things will turn out most often leads to complacency, doubt, and even "tail-spinning" where you appear to stay at the same spot. Your walk with God must be by faith. Rather than be concerned about the unknowns, focus on what you know. As you place one foot in front of the other toward your destiny, the picture will progressively unravel and become clearer.

Endurance

The journey of life toward realizing your destiny is a process that must take its course. You must take it in strides one step at a time. You cannot rush it. You need to enjoy or endure various moments of the trip and learn from the experiences you encounter. Realize that there is a time and season for everything under the sun (Ecclesiastes 3:1).

Imagine what would have happened if Moses refused to begin the journey, not having an elaborate plan, or if he had abandoned the project midway. He had every reason to quit as Pharaoh got tired of seeing him, particularly when he said to Moses: "'Get away from me! Take heed to yourself and see my face no more! For in the day you see my face you shall die!'" (Exodus 10:28). Moses would not relent because he heard from God and placed greater premium on God's voice than on Pharaoh's voice.

God has a great plan for your life. He has vested interest in your success, irrespective of your background, experience, heritage, race, or gender. He knew you before you were formed in your mother's womb, predestined you, called you, and desires to help you realize your destiny. However, within the framework of destiny, you have a role to play. You have to walk with God and accept His plans – in humble submission.

What would history have recorded if Moses held onto Pharaoh's threat as an excuse not to go further in the quest to fulfill his destiny? Are there some excuses you are holding onto for not fulfilling your destiny? How about dropping those excuses and beginning to walk with God by faith? How about heeding the call and promptings of God for you? Where your will is weak, would you ask God to strengthen your will? Know that you have all it takes to accomplish God's plans for your life. He has deposited it in you. Your God-given capabilities, gifts, and talents are there for you to utilize.

Destiny framework exercise:

1. Spend some time pondering the direction you truly believe God wants your life to take. Consider the things that you're

interested in, passionate about, and inspired to accomplish in life. What do you see yourself doing that would bring God glory and give you fulfillment?

2. Identify the stumbling blocks and limitations that are stopping you from pursuing God's plans?

3. What steps, actions, decisions, or changes can you set in motion today to overcome those stumbling blocks?

Chapter Three:

Levels of Destiny Operations

"Now there are diversities of gifts … And there are differences of administrations, and there are diversities of operations… But all these worketh that one and the selfsame Spirit, dividing to every man severally as He will."
– I Corinthians 12:4-11 (KJV)

"To accomplish our destiny it is not enough to merely guard prudently against road accidents. We must also cover before nightfall the distance assigned to each of us."
– Alexis Carrel

Destiny operates at individual and corporate levels. At the individual level it is God's premeditated outcome, purpose, and calling for an individual. Each person has a unique mission that God has for him to accomplish.

At the corporate level, God has similarly premeditated the destiny of a collective people at national, regional, family, and organizational levels. Individual and corporate levels of destiny are interconnected as we see throughout the Scriptures.

Corporate and individual destinies share similar factors that help bring about fulfillment. However, there are peculiar features that cannot be ignored. Individual destiny pertains to an individual's calling that will inevitably need the input of others for fulfillment. Corporate destiny involves the divine plan for a collective group or body of people whose potential success, or shortcoming, is determined by the group's collective performance, as opposed to just one individual's performance. In a corporate movement toward destiny,

effective leadership cannot be overemphasized. Leadership structures in a corporate body should recognize that everyone has a role
to play in the outcome of the group as a whole. Consequently, mech-
anisms should be deliberately put in place to help each individual
contribute positively toward the success of the body as a whole,
while eliminating factors that lead to disintegration, discouragement, and low group morale.

At the individual level we can see the paths of Moses' destiny
unravel and merge onto the major highway of Israel's collective
destiny as a nation. God raised up and groomed Moses for certain
purposes related to and interwoven with His foreordained purpose
for Israel corporately. As for corporate Israel, God took them
through a period of preparation – from enslavement and oppression
under Egypt's hard rule to becoming a great nation in the Promised
Land that flowed with milk and honey. The principles for success
in the path leading to individual or corporate destinies are similar.
Individuals who have discovered what God is calling them to do
will embark on initiatives that have eternal impact on the corporate
destinies of their communities.

When God calls you, He knows the experiences you will encounter in the course of your calling beforehand. For instance, God knew
ahead of time that Israel would come to the Red Sea when they left
Egypt. He also knew they would come to the bitter water of Marah
and encounter other obstacles along their path. He knew about the
challenges they would face and made provision for each one well
ahead of those experiences. God chose not to alert them ahead of
time, and that was His prerogative.

As with Moses and Israel, God sees the crossroads and challenges of your life ahead of time and may choose to permit you to
encounter them. While you would naturally prefer to have a smooth
sailing, there are inherent benefits to experiencing the trials of life.
You will need to embrace life's challenges in order to discover their
benefits. This is how the apostle James relates the benefits of challenges: "My brethren, count it all joy when you fall into various
trials, knowing that the testing of your faith produces patience.
But let patience have its perfect work, that you may be perfect and
complete, lacking nothing" (James 1:2-4).

With the right attitude and perspective, the hidden and glorious benefits in every distasteful experience of life can be discovered. In James' words, you need to *"count it all joy."* That was the same attitude that allowed Paul to make enormous impact in his calling, even during times of unprecedented difficulties, opposition, and imprisonment. He was able to spend time in prayer, in evangelizing to the house of Caesar, as well as writing the epistles for the encouragement of many generations that would read about his experiences afterwards.

With a right attitude and perspective, the psalmist said: "It is good for me that I have been afflicted, that I may learn Your statutes" (Psalm 119:71). Your insight into the benefits of afflictions is an important determinant of your ability to continually draw closer to your destiny. Complaining and holding onto past memories, wishing you were back where you once were, will serve no useful purpose but stall your progress and the achievement of your destiny. Instead, be poised to face momentary issues head-on, putting your trust in God and letting Him be your Guide. You can never tell what you will encounter in the journey of life, but rest assured that God knows and will always make provision for those challenges.

In Exodus 17:1-7 God led corporate Israel to Rephidim where there was no water. God wished that they had learned obedience and trust, but no. They would have advanced at a faster pace if they had stopped doubting God and murmuring against their leaders and about where they were. The sooner you learn obedience—putting your trust in God and demonstrating that you are trustworthy—the sooner you will find out that God will not need to test you repeatedly on the same issues. Instead, the smoother your journey to destiny will be. It is unheard of for a student to be held back and subjected to repeat testing after passing a standardized test that determines their readiness for the next class.

In the movement toward corporate destiny, God works on the leaders and followers simultaneously. With the exodus of the Israelites to the Promised Land, God was preparing Moses with leadership qualities in the course of the journey. God told Moses to gather the elders and people when He was about to perform a miracle at Rephidim. Why? Leaders need to learn to ask questions and not work on assumptions. God is purposeful, so everything He does with you and through you is for a purpose. If Moses had asked God how many plagues it would require before Pharaoh released his grip on the Israelites, or about the encounters they should expect along the way, perhaps he would have received some insight into the details of the journey. "He reveals deep and secret things" (Daniel 2:22a). We should, however, not expect to know everything, since "the secret things belong to the Lord our God" (Deuteronomy 29:29a).

In the pursuit of fulfilling your personal destiny, give careful attention to the role of others that God brings along your path. In Exodus 17, for example, Moses did not seem to inquire from God why He wanted the elders present for the miracle of bringing water from the rock. God was clearly up to something. The event was not just about the miraculous provision of water as if to convince the elders of the power of God; rather, it is highly probable that God wanted Moses to begin establishing an effective leadership structure that was critical to the accomplishment of Israel's corporate destiny.

God made a clear distinction between the elders of Israel and the people. Identifying the elders and properly assigning leadership responsibilities for easier management of the people in their transition to Canaan would make it easier for Israel to accomplish her corporate destiny and speed up the accomplishment of Moses' personal destiny. For would-be leaders and those already in positions of leadership, this principle of delegating authority and responsibilities is one that cannot be overlooked. If done properly (in conjunction with establishing clearly articulated vision, mission, core values, and strategic plans that are informed by God), people can advance further and faster corporately and individually toward realizing their destinies. Moses never sought his own glory, though he made some mistakes along the way to the Promised Land. He always put corporate Israel's interests ahead of his personal interests, and God's glory above his own.

In times of crisis, seek to be part of the solution instead of part of the problem. Do not get carried away by the magnitude of the problem. Instead, have the right attitude and resist every urge to slack off or give up. In Numbers 14:1-10 Joshua and Caleb understood the challenge before them but with the right perspective and attitude elected to be part of the solution rather than magnify the problem.

Trials and Advancement

David was anointed in 1 Samuel 16:12 but did not attain any outward form of significance until there was a crisis involving

Goliath. Again, we see an intersection between an individual's destiny and corporate destiny. David stepped up to the crisis, and his life was never the same. He followed the urge within his heart that must have been divinely inspired and guided. That urge and David's affirmative response helped elevate him personally on his destiny trail, while preserving corporate Israel's destiny.

In Romans 8:28 we are told that "All things work together for good to them that love God, to those who are the called according to His purpose." God has a brilliant way of delivering blessings in the midst of our trials. Many blessings come disguised in challenges and disappointments. Some dilemmas are orchestrated or permitted by God so that He can take our enemies unaware and bless us in the midst of them.

For example, Job's troubles started with God bragging about him. In Job 1:8 we read: "...then the Lord said to Satan, have you considered my servant Job, that there is none like him on the earth, a blameless and upright man, one who fears God and shuns evil?" God allowed Satan to afflict Job in the same way many today have been afflicted. Some wonder why they had to go through excruciating experiences, and where God was in such situations. They wonder why prayers appear to go unanswered. They ask when their breakthroughs will finally come.

If you are in such a situation, you should find it comforting to know that blessings do come in disguise. If Satan had his way, he would have killed you by now, but God has placed a limit on Satan's strike. When you go through life's struggles, bear in mind that God is up to something good that will bring blessings to you and glory to Him. After Job's storm was past, abundance of blessings—more than he had going into his storm—came (see Job 42:10-17). Put differently, blessings await us on the other side of the storms of life. However, we must recognize the blessings and take possession.

Our world is filled with great men and women who have overcome tremendous challenges in life. Where others fell by the wayside, they scaled over hurdles to achieve greatness. As an example we can look at the life of Saul, David's predecessor, who is often cast as a villain but actually started well with God and had some very good qualities that we can learn from (see 1 Samuel 9:1-19; 10:14-27; 11:1-15).

In 1 Samuel 9:3 we see that Saul's father, Kish, lost three donkeys and Saul was asked to go fetch them. This was a difficult and seemingly impossible mission. The loss of the donkeys must have been a painful and sad experience for Saul's family. Donkeys in Saul's day represented a valuable asset: the means of transportation, wealth, status, opportunities, and source of capital for business ventures. This must have been a difficult experience for both Kish and Saul. Questions must have run through their minds regarding how to go about recovering the donkeys, where to start, what to bring along in the search, and how far to go.

People today continue to lose valuable assets: investments, jobs, relationships, opportunities, and so forth. When these happen, questions of *why* well up from within. If only you knew that your crisis could very well be blessings wrapped up in disguise, then you would remain hopeful with a positive attitude rather than saddled with regrets and complaints. The Bible tells us in 1 Thessalonians 5:18 that "in everything give thanks for this is the will of God in Christ Jesus for you," and in Romans 8:28, "all things work together for good to those who love God." Some dilemmas are permitted by God for the greater good of those who love Him. Job had no clue that at the end of his trouble he would be tremendously blessed beyond his state prior to the trials. Job was wise to maintain his composure with God rather than sin against Him in the midst of his trials. You must resist every temptation to go against God in the midst of your troubles. That is the time to reassess your relationship with God and draw nearer to Him.

Saul had no clue of what was coming his way when he went about looking for his father's lost donkeys. In 1 Samuel 9:4-5 Saul searched far and wide and ran out of supplies and yet could not find those precious donkeys. This must have been quite frustrating. Every step in Saul's frustration drew him closer to his destiny, though he could not tell at the time. Similarly, when David was out caring for his father's herds, and was later sent by his father to his brothers on the battlefield where he encountered Goliath, every step of the way brought him closer to his destiny.

The trials we go through can bring us closer to our destiny if we approach them as God's Word prescribes. God remains the same yesterday, today, and forever. He does not change. What He did for others in the past, He certainly can and will do for you as well. Saul's crisis had nothing to do with donkeys. The loss of donkeys and the painful journey to recovering them were merely God's design: a setup and brilliant strategy to connect Saul with his destiny. The challenges in your life have far greater implications for your benefits than you often realize.

While Saul was going through his trials, unknown to him, God had given instructions to the prophet Samuel to anoint him as Israel's king. Meanwhile Saul was clueless but walked in obedience to his father. Along the way Saul was connected to Samuel, who would help further the realization of his destiny. The challenges of life more often than not do not consist of the things that meet the natural eyes. So our primary challenge is with gaining understanding of the plans of God in the midst of difficulties. As we go through life's challenges, God reveals things to us in part and often connects us with people having other pieces of the puzzle. Those people are key enablers in our bid to fulfilling our destinies. If you must realize your destiny, therefore, you cannot afford to neglect, disregard or abuse the people — however insignificant they may appear — that God brings along your path. God is a master strategist at connecting you with helpers on your path to destiny.

Joseph must have been seen as irrelevant to Pharaoh and the kingdom of Egypt when he was slaving in Potiphar's house and later imprisoned for an offense he did not commit, yet God was preparing to use the situations to fulfill his destiny, as well as use him to advance the fulfillment of Pharaoh's destiny in preserving the lives of God's people and His kingdom. Here's another example of individual destiny influencing the realization of corporate destiny. Naaman is described as a "great and honorable man" in the Bible. He would have died prematurely of leprosy if the seemingly unimportant young maidservant did not come to his rescue (see 2 Kings 5).

Talking about relationships, in 1 Samuel 9:6 Saul's servant provided vital counsel and assistance that brought Saul closer to his destiny at a point when Saul was about to give up on his expedition. The need to appreciate the people God brings across our paths cannot be overemphasized. Relationships come in different shapes and forms: spouses, children, clergy, colleagues, staff, subordinates, volunteers, neighbors, and even strangers. God uses people to fulfill His plans for our lives and to draw us closer to our destinies. We learn some helpful truths from the experiences of Saul and David as follows:

Obedience: They both obeyed their fathers. They observed the commandment to honor parents (Exodus 20:12). This will be discussed at greater length later in a subsequent chapter. They both took instructions from their fathers and did what they were instructed to do (1 Samuel 9:3; 17:17-22). In like manner, we should be obedient to authority, particularly our parents, authentic ministers, and most importantly our heavenly Father.

Honor: Saul regarded and honored his father (Kish) and God's servant, the prophet Samuel, even when he had no prior relationship with him. Honoring genuine servants of God portrays honor for God Himself (1 Samuel 9:7, Matthew 25:37-40). Likewise, David honored his father as well as God's servants every step of his journey to destiny.

Focus: Saul was focused while looking for the lost donkeys, particularly when he saw the young women during his search (1 Samuel 9:11). What would Solomon have done under those circumstances? Some men easily lose focus when they see women, while the loss of focus for others may result from an unhealthy pursuit of money, material gains, or exposure to fleeting fame. David was one of the faith-worthies that perfected the art of focus all through his life. Be focused and do not lose sight of your destiny.

Attitude: Saul maintained a positive attitude and mannerisms. He was polite. Imagine him saying "please" when he came to Samuel to enquire about the seer after a long and exhausting search that ordinarily would have made him moody. Good manners and positive attitude are like sweet fragrance. They will draw people to you and help accelerate your progress toward the realization of your destiny. It is necessary to periodically self-evaluate our attitudes and mannerisms so that we can work on them as needed (see 1 Samuel 9:18; 17:28-30).

Patience and humility: Both Saul and David started off being patient and humble. Saul's humility (1 Samuel 9:22-24) was an essential quality that lifted him up before all Israel. When Saul lost these qualities, he lost his destiny as king over God's people. The Bible says in James 4:10 to "humble yourself in the sight of the Lord and He will lift you up." David demonstrated humility as can be observed when his oldest brother addressed him roughly (1 Samuel 17:28-30) and when persecuted by Saul.

Confidentiality: When Saul's uncle, a busybody, was trying to extract information from him, Saul applied wisdom in not disclosing divine revelation of what God was doing in his life and the nation of Israel. Be a good steward of confidential information, including divine revelation from God. Be careful of who, when, and the extent, if at all, with which you disclose confidential divine revelations from God.

Triumph follows trials

God used the problem of lost donkeys to bring Saul to a place where he was anointed Israel's king (1 Samuel 10:9). Sometimes it might take multiple problems to get the lesson through to us — as it did with Saul and David. Life is full of trials. For instance, in 1 Samuel 11:5 King Saul was still working in the field rearing animals until another challenge arose in which the Ammonites came up against Jabesh Gilead and caused the people to cry and weep. But this time God had another grand plan. He stirred up Saul's anger and gave him a strategy to defeat the Ammonites, who fell under his leadership. It took multiple trials for Saul and David to get to their leadership destiny. God is Master at giving grace at such times (James 4:6, Proverbs 3:34). When God intervenes in your life, those who previously despised you will be compelled to honor you, sing your praises, and glorify God.

In order to triumph in trial, we must face trials head-on, not shy away from them. Nelson Mandela, Martin Luther King, Harriet Tubman, Abraham Lincoln and W.E.B. Du Bois are among several people that faced the issues of their day head-on and were elevated in times of crisis. The ability to provide solutions to challenges faced by people or to simplify life for people often provides avenues to leave significant footprints. When you come across difficulties as you continue your life's journey toward becoming all that God has purposed for you, you must find out the hidden opportunities in them. Pay attention to your urges and propensities amidst crises and do not suppress them – if they are in the interest of common good. Take stock of the gifts and talents that you bring to bear, and use them to provide solutions to problems facing people. You were made to be a light to those in darkness. There should be something about your life that shines and leaves a lasting positive impact on others.

Destiny cannot be fulfilled in a vacuum. Destiny must be realized where others can be impacted for good. If you know of ways to impact the lives of others for good, do it. If you know how you could make a difference in the world, go for it.

In Exodus 3:11-22 and 4:1-17, Moses felt inadequate because of the enormity of the mission God was calling him to fulfill. Even the best of us may feel inadequate when faced with challenges that are daunting and overwhelming. We all have weaknesses and limitations, but we can learn to work on strengthening and managing those weak spots through partnership, collaboration, and submission. We cannot allow our weaknesses to determine what we do or do not do. We must instead discover our areas of strength and use them, while our areas of weakness should be addressed through strategic partnership and collaboration. Unmanaged weaknesses, especially those pertaining to behavioral and moral traits, can hinder the fulfillment of our destinies if they go unchecked.

One effective way to correct our weaknesses is by working with others who possess strength in the areas of our weaknesses. God often sends such people to help us – if we are sincere enough and will look for help. An example of getting help in an area of weakness is Moses' collaboration with his elder brother Aaron, who was led by God to be Moses' spokesman in order to compensate for Moses' speech deficiency. At another time, Jethro, Moses' father in-law, was there to provide Moses with invaluable counsel on how to lead the people effectively through delegation of responsibilities so that Moses could spend more time in his primary calling, and to increase his capacity for a lasting impact among his people (Exodus 18:18-20). In the early church, the apostles reached a decision to delegate responsibilities to the deacons while they spent more time on their primary responsibilities to pray and study the Word (Acts 6:2-4).

When the operation of the essentials for achieving destiny is fraught with weaknesses that are not open to partnership and collaboration, a leader may never reach the level of accomplishment that God has in mind. Collaborating with others and letting them help in the areas of our weaknesses enables us to be more effective. Accommodating the temptation to be all things to all people will thinly spread your reach and diminish your effectiveness in life's endeavors. Think corporately, involve others, empower them where necessary, and delegate responsibilities where required. Identify your core strengths and primary calling, and be certain to explore them to the utmost.

Leadership and Destiny

In a corporate setting, people can collectively progress toward a desired outcome or be doomed together. When Israel sinned against God and was punished, everyone suffered, and when they received grace and advanced, everyone benefited.

In 1 Corinthians 12 the apostle Paul noted that we are members of one body, which means that Christians have mutually beneficial relationships and a collective eternal destiny as a body of believers. In order for the overall body to flourish within any given organized body of believers, it is vital that the unique gifts and talents of each member are identified and properly aligned with suitable functions for the benefit of the body as a whole.

Albert Einstein is believed to have said: "Everybody is a genius. But if you judge a fish by its ability to climb a tree, it will live its whole life believing that it is stupid." Effective leadership engages in systematic processes that foster the discovery of each person's unique gift, followed by the deployment of those gifts to areas where they provide the most value to the organization as a whole. As the entire unit is built up, each believer can then draw benefits directly or indirectly from the corporate body – as supplied by other members of the body. With poor leadership, the body will fail to attain to its optimum potentials. Leadership can be seen as the brain, which functions to provide information and feedback to every part of the body as needed.

Leadership is the unit where vision and mission are clearly defined, articulated, and managed. It is at this level that information is disseminated to the people comprising the corporate body as a whole, and feedback is received. When feedback received points to problems, it is necessary, under good leadership, to provide timely solutions to facilitate health and growth of the body. Resolving issues on time helps keep the corporate body on track to fulfillment, while neglect undermines the corporate health and success.

43

In moving a corporate body toward its destiny, we can learn a lot from Moses and the people in the Exodus narrative. Moses could not possibly have done it all by himself. No leader can. It is a matter of time before they run into difficulties. When chaos intensified in Exodus 17:4, Moses cried to God. In response, "the LORD said to Moses, go on before the people, and take with you some of the elders of Israel. Also take in your hand your rod with which you struck the river, and go" (Exodus 17:5). Here we find that Moses was to lead collaboratively with some elders. In this instance, the role of an elder is not a function of age but of experience and responsibilities.

In Paul's epistles to Timothy and Titus, the qualifications of an elder are spelled out (see 1 Timothy 3:1-12 and Titus 1:5-9). When selecting leaders, consideration must be given only to those who are cut out for the leadership responsibilities and functions that will be assumed. In Exodus 17:9 Moses told Joshua to choose some men to fight against Amalek while he (Moses) stood on the hill with the rod of God in his hand. It became obvious that the challenge encountered a few days earlier in Rephidim was probably a blessing in disguise. It provided Moses the opportunity to identify leaders for the challenge that was soon to follow. It was at Rephidim that Moses identified Joshua and other leaders with which to share the burden of leading the people. It turned out that Joshua was the one who led Israel in combat against Amalek while Moses, Aaron, and Hur went to the hilltop to commune with God.

An effective leadership structure gave Moses the ability to see how his people were faring in battle and to make adjustments for their collective good. What's more, he had the staff in his hand and enforced his overall spiritual authority from this vantage point. What interplay of physical and spiritual phenomena! Moses and Israel would never have succeeded in this battle if Moses had attempted to do it all by himself, or if his vision was limited while entrenched in the forefront of battle.

Transparency and Information Sharing

In Exodus 17:14 God instructed Moses to "write this for a memorial in the book and recount it in the hearing of Joshua, that [He] will utterly blot out the remembrance of Amalek from under heaven." Effective leadership involves transparency and information sharing, especially amongst those at the leadership level. The leaders in Israel needed information to be effective. Important information cannot be hoarded by leaders from others on their team. If the leaders on your team cannot be trusted with key information, perhaps they do not belong there in the first place! "Can two walk together, unless they are agreed?" (Amos 3:3). God in His abundant wisdom instructed the prophet Habakkuk to "Write the vision and make it *plain* on tablets, that he may run who reads it" (Habakkuk 2:2).

Effective leaders are often good stewards of information. As a result of fear, betrayal of trust, and negative experiences, some keep tight rein over information where it is appropriate to share. It is rather unfortunate that some in leadership positions hoard information as a means of undue manipulation and control in what can be described as a "Jezebel spirit." God Himself models transparency: "Surely the Lord God does nothing unless He reveals His secret to His servants and the prophets" (Amos 3:7). When God was on the verge of destroying Sodom, He was transparent with His trusted servant Abraham about whom He said, "shall I hide from Abraham what I am doing?" (Genesis 18:18). Transparency promotes trust, loyalty, and relational cohesion.

In Jesus' leadership approach, He spoke to the crowd in parables concerning information He did not want them to grasp, but with His disciples He spoke plainly and shared key information (Matthew 13:10-13) similar to what God asked Moses to do. One way of looking at poor communication between leaders and those on the leadership team in particular and the body in general, is by considering the effect of the brain not communicating with the rest of the body. When this happens, there is bound to be sickness and dysfunction in the body as a whole. The body cannot perform at optimum level and may sooner or later be retired six feet underground.

Your response to your destiny framework:
1. How would you describe the current trajectory of your individual destiny?

2. Where do you fit in the accomplishment of corporate destiny (such as church, business organization, or other communities to which you belong)?

3. If you are called to be a leader, what are your personal as-

sessments of your strengths? How do they compare to how others perceive your strengths?

4. If you are a leader, what are your perceived weaknesses and others' observation of your weaknesses? What can you do to put those weaknesses in check? (This may require getting a mentor, partnering or collaborating with someone who is strong in your area of weakness, or hiring someone to help you).

Chapter Four:

Free Will

"For it is God who works in you both to will and to do of His good pleasure."
– Philippians 2:13

"What is the highest secret to victory and peace? To will what God wills, and strike a league with destiny."
– William R. Alge

E veryone has free will. But freedom of choice has its limits. In order to excel in the journey to your God-ordained destiny, you will have to recognize the limitations of your freedom. You always have a choice to do whatever you want, but to fulfill your destiny those choices have to be in accordance with God's plan for your life; otherwise you might be on a long hard road to "nowhere." The extent to which you permit external forces and the context within which you exercise your will have an overarching effect on your destiny.

On the path to fulfilling your destiny, you need to appreciate the fact that free will has limitations and can only be successfully exercised within predefined boundaries, appropriate environment, and conditions that permit your will to be expressed for the furtherance of God's plan and purpose. A person's free will is shaped by laws, which in turn are shaped by practices, values, social norms, and beliefs. In every society where there is rule of law, free will can be exercised to a person's benefit when the rights of others are not violated, and to a person's detriment when the rights of others are violated.

If free will were without parameters, there would be no need for prisons. Men and women could decide to live lifestyles as they saw fit instead of what the law prescribes and permits—but the consequences could be devastating. Yet, in spite of the importance of human laws that emerge to guide free will, they remain imperfect, made to suit the desires of the majority, and are often flawed.

Different communities, for example, have differing views on homosexuality, terrorism, polygamy, and other important moral issues. Some practices may be acceptable in certain communities while forbidden in others. It is possible for someone who engages in polygamy or same-sex marriage to choose to relocate from a community that does not grant permission to their lifestyle to another community that does. Similarly, if an individual chooses to use marijuana freely in Massachusetts, where the law does not support it, he would be exposing himself to the grim force of the law. However, he has the free will to relocate to California or Amsterdam where he could have judicial acceptance.

Furthermore, while a native New Yorker might not engage in a pluralistic marriage because of his observance of the laws prohibiting it and the social issues associated with polygamy, his counterpart in a place like Utah or Nigeria might not find such culture offensive. The same native New Yorker who would oppose pluralistic marriage might find himself in intimate relationships and affairs with multiple partners without adverse consequences, outside the context of marriage. He may even decide not to get married in an effort to avoid the marriage constraints that would prohibit him from exercising free will in this context. All of these are to support the fact that differing conclusions could be drawn on similar acts by the same people, depending on the context.

It is important that we pay close attention to external forces or influences—both good and bad—that impose upon our will and destiny so that we do not let them distract us from fulfilling our destiny. Unlike human laws that evolve, God's laws are perfect, universal, and remain the same – past, present, and future. God rules over the universe and His laws supersede those established by popular demand. A man in his right senses cannot momentarily, in the exercise of his free will, decide to make his permanent abode under the sea. He may choose to live in a submarine submerged at sea for a period of time. However, not being an aquatic creature, he could not stay beyond the time that the submarine engine would support, or he could be heading for disaster.

When conditions are conducive for the expression of one's free will, and desires for preferred outcomes are complementary to the will of God, then one is on track to fulfilling his destiny.

Every bad desire can be traced to unchecked self-will, the devil, and his agents. The devil's avowed will and objective, which can find expression through our choices, is to destroy our destiny. Godly desires, on the other hand, emanate from God and are intended to steer us in the right paths to our destiny. These find expression as well through our choices. In Philippians 2:13, the Bible says that "For God is working in you, giving you the desire and the power to do what pleases him" (NLT). God enables us to make the right choices by His Spirit. We choose to let Him, or on the contrary refuse Him and choose the devil's promptings.

An excellent determinant of whether you are in the right path is to compare your desires with the Word of God. God will not give you desires that contradict His Word. Similarly, the means by which you act upon your God-given desires should reflect God's values. The end does not always justify the means. God's law and people should never be violated in the process of achieving God's purposes.

God has established parameters within which we should exercise our free will and in the context of human laws that are designed for common good. While human laws are imperfect and subordinate to God's laws, God provides in His laws that we obey the laws of the land; certainly not at the expense of His laws, which help keep us on the right path to our destiny, but along with them.

The first African American president, Barack Obama, was elected at an unprecedented time when it was widely inconceivable for a minority to attain such a position of power and influence in the United States. The context was conducive for a significant change to occur, and the Constitution made provision for an American born in the United States to run for president, irrespective of race, gender, religious beliefs, parents' origin, and so forth. Though he did not initially aspire for the office, his paths were ordered in such a way that opportunities brought him closer and closer to this phase in his destiny.

The proper exercise of his free will in my view helped him become what God planned for him to be. He was well educated and acquired relevant skills as a community organizer and senator. Unlike in preceding elections, the citizens of the United States were tired of the status quo and wanted something radically different. Barack Obama talked, looked, walked, and acted differently from the status quo and also had the right people to nudge him onto the path to becoming president. Our destinies have ways of seeking us out even when we are unaware of destiny making opportunities or how to respond.

As you travel the pathways of your destiny, you might be compelled by circumstances and opportunities to make detours you had not preconceived, and to embrace ideas, insights, and dreams you never imagined. Somehow with the right context, circumstances, and opportunities, life steers you in the right, often narrow, paths that ultimately lead to the fulfillment of another crucial phase in your destiny. At such times, irrespective of the challenges, you must seek to align your will with God's will. You must muster the courage to follow your God-ordained path. For Barack Obama, the time was right, the opportunity was present, he had the right resources (mainly people), in conjunction with courage, and he went on to make history.

There is a misconception about predestination, that everything is predetermined and controlled by God, including our actions, choices, and decisions, and that we do not have any part to play in the outcome of our lives. This extreme position simply and inadvertently suggests that there is no free will. Whereas God is truly omniscient, knowing all things, there are choices we must make at different points in our pathways to destiny. It is possible that while God steers us toward the paths of our destiny, as the Spirit of God did with Jesus prior to commencing His earthly ministry, Satan works to steer us away by enticing us with appealing offers and tempting us to act against God's will, as he did with Jesus in Matthew 4:1-11. It is left to us in the exercise of free will to determine who to obey – God or Satan.

God could not have made the choice for Adam and Eve to disobey Him by eating from the tree of the knowledge of good and evil – Genesis 3. They were tempted and exercised their free will to yield to Satan's promptings instead of obeying God. Unfortunately they exercised their free will to their detriment. In Matthew 4, when Jesus Christ was also faced with conflicting choices, He chose to listen to and obey the promptings of God - His Father.

In the Garden of Gethsemane, while entering the final phase of His destiny, Jesus experienced conflict between His will and the Father's will. He made the right choice: "He went a little farther and fell on His face, and prayed, saying, 'O My Father, if it is possible, let this cup pass from Me; nevertheless, not as I will, but as You will'" (Matthew 26:39). We can learn much from Jesus' attitude and submission in the exercise of free will. Jesus' preference was to bypass the cup (representing His crucifixion), and His Father would not compel Him anyway. "Again, a second time, He went away and prayed, saying, 'O My Father, if this cup cannot pass away from Me unless I drink it, Your will be done'" (Matthew 26:42). His Father's will was clear, so He yielded to the Father and fulfilled His glorious destiny in a perfect alignment of His free will to God's plan and purpose.

Whenever we go against God's will for our lives, we are derailed from the path of our destiny (Deuteronomy 5:32, 28:14; Joshua 1:7, 23:6). It is never advisable to swim against the tide. You cannot continue to drive on the wrong side of the road and delude yourself of safety. It might not be long before the reality of a mishap teaches you otherwise.

Anyone desiring to fulfill God's chosen path for him must know God's will and align his will with God's will. In order to have an enduring success, our will must complement God's will. Where there is conflict between God's will and our will, we owe it to God to surrender our will just as Jesus did, otherwise we will end up frustrated and unfulfilled.

The exercise of our will within the context of God's will helps us stay on the path to fulfillment. Our free will and God's perfect will have direct relationship on our paths to fulfilling destiny. The more aligned our will is to the will of God, the more certain we are of fulfilling our destiny and enjoying the peace of God. Conversely, the further our will is from God's will, the harder it gets to fulfill our destiny. It is helpful to know that in all these situations God has the ability and willingness to use our past mistakes for our good, if we yield our will to His. Romans 8:28 tells us that "all things work together for the good of those who love God." God can and will often use our past mistakes and misfortunes for our good, if we allow Him.

Your Freewill assessment and action plan:
1. List the paths you are currently on that you consider contrary to God's will, based on God's Word.

2. To the best of your knowledge, what paths (pursuits, initiatives) do you believe God wants you to embrace?

3. Make a determined decision to abandon contrary paths and prayerfully begin to pursue your God-ordained paths without procrastinating.

Chapter Five:

Resources

"The earth is the lord's, and all its fullness, the world and those who dwell therein."
– Psalm 24:1

"A little faith will bring your soul to heaven, but a lot of faith will bring heaven to your soul."
– Martin Luther King Jr.

In Luke 9:2-4 Jesus commissioned His disciples "to preach the kingdom of God and to heal the sick. And He said to them, 'Take nothing for the journey, neither staffs nor bag nor bread nor money; and do not have two tunics apiece. Whatever house you enter, stay there, and from there depart.'" Simply put, Jesus' disciples were sent out empty-handed on a significant mission that undoubtedly required some resources. In response to Jesus' commission, the disciples "went out" (Luke 9:6) – with no resource to depend on. That's amazing venture with assurance of provision along the way.

Called with Limited Resources

Vital concerns that many often have when they are about to embark on the path to their God-given destiny and preferred future usually pertain to *lack* and *inadequacy*. Perceived lack of resources and inadequacy in the areas of capabilities (skills, talent, and experience) can have crippling effects on efforts at pursuing destiny. Humanly, resources are limited and are most often in short supply, but not so with God.

God has limitless supply of gifting and resources. He is the Creator of everything and owns all the resources there are. He chooses how to distribute and/or redistribute resources as He sees fit. God created the earth and all that is in it (Psalm 24:1, 1 Corinthians 10:26). He owns the silver and the gold (Haggai 2:8), as well as the cattle on a thousand hills (Psalm 50:10). What's more, He knows the ending from the beginning and has made adequate provision for the time in between. He created you with a premeditated outcome (destiny) and purpose in mind, as well as all that you need to fulfill your destiny.

Rather than get stuck and overwhelmed about lack of resources and perceived inabilities and deficiencies of the requisite needs to fulfill your destiny, trust in God. Have unequivocal faith in Him to see to it that you fulfill your destiny. God is faithful and provides all that is needed for us to succeed, if we will follow His plan for our lives. God said: "I will make you..." (Matthew 4:19); "It is your Father's good pleasure to give you the kingdom..." (Luke 12:32); and "I will build My church..." (Matthew 16:18). If you will follow Him, and are faithful to Him in all things, He surely will take responsibility over you and provide what you need to accomplish all He has set out to do in and through you.

Resources can be internal and intangible (e.g. talents, intellect, experiences, gifting) or external and tangible (e.g. people, money, real property). Irrespective of the form or the particular resources you need to realize your destiny, they are all within God's provision. Think of God as CEO and chief visionary of the entire universe. He has a vision for the world and for the people in it. God is in charge of the universe, which includes the earth and other planetary creations, and He takes full responsibility for His premeditated outcome for those that follow Him. As CEO, He chooses managers (people including you, me, and everyone that walks the earth) to accomplish specific tasks while providing the necessary resources (tangible and intangible) to accomplish assigned tasks.

The concern should therefore not so much focus on the resources, but rather on what your task is. Once we know what our task is— what we are called to do—and begin to work toward it, it is amazing how God makes the resources available in ways that are often unexpected. Moreover it becomes easier to pray for specific resources and get answers as you pray according to His will (see James 4:3).

I encourage you to ask: What am I called to do? Within God's master-plan, in what area am I expected to function? If I could summarize my destiny for this and/or the next phase of my life in one sentence, what would it be? Once you identify your calling, take baby steps, beginning with the resources you currently have while simultaneously asking God for the resources needed to accomplish it, and being on the lookout for God's provision each step of the way.

After affirming his faith in the ability of Jesus Christ, Peter was reassured by Jesus that the church would be built and the gates of hell could not prevail against it (Matthew 16:18).

When God chooses people, He selects those in whom He has deposited the necessary talents, skills, and abilities for fulfilling the given tasks – even though in measure (2 Corinthians 10:13, Ephesians 4:7). You can rest assured that the measure of resources He deposited in you will be sufficient to accomplish your destiny. Yet He gives you the ability to trade with the measure and to increase therewith. He knows you better than you know yourself, since you were created by Him anyway, and He already deposited specific gifts and talents in you. God aligns your talents, gifts, and abilities with the specific purposes for which He created you, which is the reason many people experience confusion, frustration, and lack of fulfillment when they deviate from their divine purpose.

In the parable of the talents, Jesus tells us that "the kingdom of heaven is like a man traveling to a far country, who called his own servants and delivered his goods to them. And to one he gave five talents, to another two, and to another one, to each according to his own ability; and immediately he went on a journey..." (Matthew 25:14-29).

Some key lessons we can learn from this parable are:
- God is the kingdom owner and initiates the calling and various stages of our destiny
- He provides the resources when He calls
- He disburses resources according to our abilities – known to Him
- When we prove to be faithful stewards of the limited resources He gives us, and fulfill what He asks us to do, He entrusts us with greater responsibilities/opportunities

- Conversely, if we are unfaithful stewards of the resources He gives us, He retracts what He has given us and disburses it to someone else to steward
- We could not go without the consequence of our negligence

Notice that the servants who embraced their responsibilities and put their talents to use were entrusted with more, while the servant that shied away from his responsibility and remained complacent was reprimanded.

Setting Off with Available Resources

God has deposited a measure of talents in you. As you heed your calling and take a leap of faith in the direction of your calling, you should discover your God-given talents. As you discover the talents, you cannot afford to let them lie dormant or be neglected as the servant with one talent in the parable did. You must begin to put your talents to use. Certainly there is never a lack of resources for those called by God to function in the capacity that He has called them.

The stories of Jesus getting money from the mouth of a fish to pay taxes (Matthew 17:27), the feeding of five thousand with five loaves of bread and two small fish (Luke 9:16), and several others serve to prove that God has all the resources for the fulfillment of our calling – if we will trust Him. Better still, it goes further to reassure us that God takes responsibility for providing the resources and will meet our needs even from the least likely sources.

Of all the external and tangible resources that God gives, human beings remain the most important. Little wonder that Satan finds that same resource as the most targeted object of his assaults. That is why marriages are under increasing attacks, and family feuds leading to separation are at an unprecedented high. People are marginalized and exploited in communities and workplaces. Unforgiveness, bitterness, backbiting, backstabbing, and similar other vices have replaced genuine care and affection toward one another. Satan is no doubt on the prowl against God's most treasured resource – people.

God commands us to love Him and love our neighbors as ourselves. Loving our neighbors cuts across every imaginable relationship and underscores the value that must be placed on fellow humans. People are a key success factor in the journey to destiny.

Jesus said to Peter "…upon this rock I will build my church…" (Matthew 16:18). Whether "this" refers to the faith of Peter or the person of Simon Peter as some theologians would want to split hairs is immaterial. Both the person and the faith of Peter are not mutually exclusive for the truth Jesus wanted to convey. Jesus was going to use the person of Peter (tangible) as well as his faith (intangible) to advance the kingdom of God just as He would for all people.

Even though people are incredibly valuable and important in God's master plan, they must never be treated as means to an end, or as commodities to be used to advance personal agenda. Only God has the prerogative to do with us as He deems fit. However, God strategically positions people on the pathways of their destiny (individual or corporate) to help bring about fulfillment.

Engaging Human Resources

Abraham had a tremendous promise of God on his life but needed Sarah to birth Isaac (the type of God's "only begotten") and his servants as an army and helpers round about him – all in God's designed plan to fulfill Abraham's destiny.

Similarly, God placed Zipporah his wife, Aaron his brother, Jethro his father-in-law, and Joshua his successor in the life of Moses in order to advance his destiny. He also placed the wise elders in whom God shared Moses' spirit (Numbers 11:16-25), and many others. Other biblical examples include Paul and his protégés (Timothy, Titus, etc.), Ruth and Naomi, Elijah and Elisha, Mordecai and Esther, Jesus Christ and His disciples, and several others living and dead.

A common challenge in the path to our destiny is the ease by which we become conceited and self-centered when we begin to experience some level of success. We so soon forget that we are on a mission ordained by God. We fail to realize and celebrate the people that God has strategically placed in our lives to help us accomplish our destinies. You will do well never to allow yourself to fall into this trap nor to take anyone for granted.

One of Moses' greatest accomplishments was the building of the tabernacle of meeting, which Moses lacked the architectural and other building skills to accomplish by himself. God said to him, "Behold, I Myself have taken your brethren the Levites from among the children of Israel; they are a gift to you, given by the LORD, to do the work of the tabernacle of meeting" (Numbers 18:6).

God gives people that He has prepared to help us fulfill our destinies. We need to see such people as precious gifts – whether they are in our family, in the church, in business, in our community, in our school, and so forth. We need to watch out for them as destiny helpers from God and engage them to help us go further, while in reciprocity we also help them go further. God, for example, gave Moses specific skilled individuals – Bezaleel and Aholiab – to further his destiny. Hear what God told Moses: "See, I have called by name Bezaleel...And I have filled him with the Spirit of God, in wisdom, in understanding, in knowledge, and in all manner of workmanship. And behold, I have given with him Aholiab..." (Exodus 31:2-3, 6).

Besides the human resources that God provides, He also makes material resources available. We can rest assured that God always has everything figured out before we even think of it, and He is only waiting for us to embark on the journey and ask (Luke 11:9-10). God sets our destiny and provides all we need to accomplish it well in advance of when those needs surface. It is amazing, for example, that before God gave Moses the instruction concerning the building of the tabernacle He had already lined up the people (Levites) as well as the materials (gold, silver, etc.) necessary to complete the project. All Moses needed to do was obey and embrace his responsibilities.

Additionally, everyone called by God to accomplish a specific mandate must be a good steward of the resources that God gives and in particular the people. Starting at home, husbands must value their wives, and wives their husbands. Children owe parents respect and care as parents themselves fulfill parental roles. Friends have the duty of faithfulness and authenticity to their friends, as some of Job's friends did with Job. Leaders must mentor and disciple those entrusted by God to their care, not taking advantage of them. We all must understand that God's calling transcends any individual person and that our destinies can only be fulfilled when our relationship with the people is void of infidelity, insecurity, politicking, and self-seeking desires.

To be faithful and productive stewards of the human resources God gives us, effective leaders, like visionaries, must present clear vision that describes what the corporate unit (community, church, family, organization, etc.) aspires to be, while establishing proper structures that outline roles and responsibilities to help bring the vision to reality. Clearly defined vision and structures enable people to understand your aspiration and how they fit into the bigger picture. There was no doubt that God was placing emphasis on clear vision when He told Habakkuk: "Write the vision and make it plain on tablets, that he may run who reads it" (Habakkuk 2:2). Clear vision makes the dream live beyond the dreamer.

Not only is it important to lead with clear vision, you must empower others in order for them to help you fulfill your destiny. A few great people are remembered today and recorded in history for their indelible footprints here on earth, while others have been long forgotten. The primary difference between those who left lasting legacies and those that are forgotten has been in their *clarity of vision* and *empowerment of others*.

Categories of Human Resources

To help you identify and appreciate the human resources that are available to further your destiny, the following key categories of people should be kept in mind as you come across them on your destiny pathways:

1. **Prompters:** These are people that prompt or point you toward your destiny. They see great potential in you that you may not even realize exists. They spot your rare gifts and talents and are genuinely interested in your success. Prompters want to help you birth the greatness within. They help bring clarity to fuzzy areas of your life and nudge you on to your success as necessary. Bible examples of such people are Mordecai, who pointed Queen Esther to the throne; Jethro, Moses' father-in-law, who helped Moses put an effective leadership structure in place for the growing nation of Israel; the apostle Paul, who identified spiritual leadership qualities in Timothy and Titus and mentored them for success in ministry; Eli, who recognized the call of God on Samuel and mentored him rather than become envious of him. Prompters often show up when it is time to transition to another phase in your journey to destiny by signaling a change in season. They may or may not be mentors but can play key roles in helping to further you along toward fulfilling your destiny.

To recognize the prompters in your life, pay attention to the following distinctive traits:

a. Prompters do not usually have ulterior motives, as they don't have anything to lose or gain.

b. The directions they steer you along are usually not in contradiction to the plans of God for your life.

c. Their counsel and nudging are often complementary to the direction of God for your life. While you may not have full understanding of God's plans, the sense of direction you get from prompters are generally in line with your dreams, desires, nudging, promptings, and overall sense of destiny.

d. They usually challenge you to take leaps of faith and to dare things you would otherwise not venture. Be cautious, however, of those who present lofty ideas and offers in contradiction to your God-given desires. However lofty those ideas may be, you will know intuitively and by the power of the Holy Spirit within you that their ideas are contrary to your destiny. When Jesus was about to transition into public ministry, Satan showed up with lofty offers as Jesus was concluding His forty days in the wilderness. It would have been tempting for someone undiscerning to take the bait. Jesus did not. He knew by the leading of the Holy Spirit what God sent Him to earth to do and determined not to do otherwise. When presented with lofty ideas, ponder this question: Is this in line with God's will or calling for my life? If you do not feel convinced that it is, the sooner you abandon the lofty idea, the better for your efforts at accomplishing destiny. When Jethro prompted Moses to select leaders among the people in Exodus 18:21-23, he was giving Moses an idea that aligned with God's earlier instructions to Moses in Exodus 3:16-18.

2. **Enablers**: These are people that buy into the vision God has given you. Enablers value you as a person, and more importantly, they value your vision and are "committed" to seeing

the vision or dream come to reality. They might be friends, relatives, volunteers, and subordinates with the requisite skills, talents, and tangible resources for fulfilling your destiny. In the life of Moses, Miriam, Aaron, and Joshua were among his destiny enablers. In the life of Jesus Christ, John the Baptist and His disciples were enablers.

Jesus' disciples performed delegated functions that advanced the kingdom of God by helping Him realize His mission here on earth. The Bible records that "After these things the Lord appointed seventy others also, and sent them two by two before His face into every city and place where He Himself was about to go" (Luke 10:1). Jesus' enablers prepared people and created conducive spiritual climates in advance of Jesus' arrival to minister in different cities. Enablers have also been found to be preservers of visions.

3. **Supporters:** These are your committed fans and cheerleaders. They believe in you and cheer you on to success. Because most of your supporters may not be known on a personal level, they are often overlooked. Supporters play significant roles in your advancement. Imagine the difference that energetic fans and cheerleaders often make in the sports arena. When an author's book is a bestseller, s/he receives encouragement from endorsements and repeat sales patronage from readers s/he may not know personally. When people gather to hear an inspirational speaker, they lend support and signal that they value the message by occasional cheers and affirmations. Irrespective of our calling, we all need supporters. Supporters sing your praise publicly and privately. They endorse you and what you have to offer openly as well as behind closed doors.

4. **Preservers**: These are people that run with the vision and carry on the legacy long after the pioneer has retired from their work. They are the believing disciples, the ardent followers, the protégés and apprentices that foster continuity. They are no less important than the others – prompters, enablers, and supporters. When properly mentored and empowered, they continue to keep the vision alive. Visionaries who desire that

61

their dream live past them cannot do without identifying, mentoring, and empowering preservers. Preservers, as in every relay race, must be taught how to receive, handle, and eventually pass on the baton for continuity.

Jesus trained His disciples, commissioned and instructed them to do the same. Jesus said: "Go therefore and make disciples of all the nations, baptizing them in the name of the Father and of the Son and of the Holy Spirit, teaching them to observe all things that I have commanded you; and lo, I am with you always, even to the end of the age. Amen" (Matthew 28:18-19). This was also the case when He sent them two by two in Luke 10:1.

Paul similarly said in his letter to Timothy: "And the things that you have heard from me among many witnesses, commit these to faithful men who will be able to teach others also" (2 Timothy 2:2).

Here are a few things to note in identifying preservers:

- Preservers must have the natural ability to stick with visions
- They must be people with teachable minds and not "know-it-alls"
- They must be God-fearing, not men-pleasers, people who are considered wise
- They also must be trustworthy, i.e. faithful and with integrity
- They must be selfless, not self-seeking
- They must have administrative abilities commensurate to their capability level: thousands, hundreds, etc.

Observe the qualities suggested by Jethro, Moses' father-in-law: "Moreover you shall select from all the people able men, such as fear God, men of truth, hating covetousness; and place such over them to be rulers of thousands, rulers of hundreds, rulers of fifties, and rulers of tens" (Exodus 18:21). Also see Acts 6:3-6.

Leaders need prompters, enablers, supporters, and preservers. In order to establish a lasting legacy, leaders must identify preservers with the aforementioned qualities and groom them for continuity, while putting systems or structures in place to facilitate that. Protégés should be identified and mentored well before they are left with key leadership responsibilities. Mentoring ensures proper training and gives room for evaluations and remediation before the burdens of leadership fall squarely on the mentee's shoulders. In Moses' absence, Aaron did not know what to do, which led to the building of the golden calf (Exodus 32). The lack of and/or inadequacy of mentoring is one of the reasons why we see such a great amount of leadership failure today. There has to be a deliberate attempt at grooming leaders for the future.

Addressing your resource hang-ups:

1. Identify the most important venture God asked you to begin, if any, that you haven't commenced because you are waiting for resources. Pray for faith and courage to begin, and for God to provide resources along the way.

2. Identify the resources (tangible and intangible) you currently possess. Write down action steps you can take starting with what you have. (Note: The resources may be people you can approach to help with resources you need).

Note: Concerning your calling, Lester Sumrall advises in his book *The Gifts and Ministries of the Holy Spirit* to start where you are with baby steps—it gets easier as you climb higher. He goes on to say, "Don't wait for doors to open, or you will die of old age while you are waiting! Create doors all around you. There is so much that needs to be done, so get started!"

3. Identify the different categories of human resources mentioned in this chapter that God has put in your life, where you are currently. Begin to appreciate them and permit them to help you be all that God has created you to be.

4. Pray for God to give you true and enduring resources.

Chapter Six:

Times and Seasons

"To everything there is a season, a time for every purpose under heaven."
– Ecclesiastes 3:1

"It is a mistake to try to look too far ahead. The chain of destiny can only be grasped one link at a time."
– Winston Churchill

There is an appointed time for everything in life. Understanding times and seasons is beneficial in your quest to fulfill your destiny. Understanding will help keep you from being frustrated when things are not going as you planned or expected. Understanding the concept of times and seasons keeps you from giving up your mission prematurely and helps you stay on course. When you understand the role of divine timing on your destiny, you can maintain hope while being patient and confident that your desired outcome will come to pass.

The Bible says in Lamentations 3:26 that "it is good that one should hope and wait." Hope keeps your focus on your expected destination, while patience helps keep you on course until the time of actualization. There is a set time and season for the fulfillment of the key events you are waiting to see unravel in your life.

Long before it happened, God told Abraham that his descendants would spend four hundred years in Egypt after which they would experience the exodus (see Genesis 15:13-14). Known or unknown to the Israelites, God had a set time for their entrance into, enslavement in, and exit out of Egypt. And when their exit time was up, again God had made preparation for the man Moses, the deliverer, to lead the exit. Moses himself could not do the deliverance by his power or influence. There was timing for everything: from the birth of the deliverer, to the exit from Egypt's bondage, to the journey through the Red Sea and the wilderness, to the arrival at the Promised Land.

On their exit, God instructed Moses: "speak now to the hearing of all the people, and let every man and woman ask of all his or her neighbor..." (Exodus 11:2). In verse 3, we read that the Lord gave the people favor in the sight of all the Egyptians. God determined the timing of their exit: a time when their enemies would turn around to favor them, just as He orders the events of our lives at the right timing when we let Him.

To Moses, God instructed: *"Speak now."* Speaking the same message at any other time would not have produced the same result. Asking their enemies for silver and gold at the height of "hate" would naturally have been inconceivable, but not when God is calling the shots – it was the perfect timing. Moses and all of Israel knew it and obeyed. When God is involved in your journey to destiny, He will order the timing.

On our pathways to destiny, there is a place for prior experiences – good or bad. None of life's experiences goes to waste. The Israelites would never have listened to Moses, or mustered the courage to make such audacious requests of their neighbors and masters, had they not observed the nine plagues (up until that time) that God inflicted on the Egyptians. Those experiences gave credibility to Moses' calling as a servant of God and boosted their confidence in God's ability to do the unthinkable. The past prepares you for future events, which can have significant impact on your destiny if you are discerning and seize the moments.

You may have accomplished some great feats in life and may also have been faced with some intimidating failures. The fact that you are alive is a notable miracle when you consider the odds you have overcome knowingly or unknowingly. You may already know, for example, that several million sperms competed for your place in the race to the ovary, but you prevailed in your mother's womb over millions. Many fetuses did not make it to the world, while several others that made it died of complications at birth or

65

at tender ages. You are here! You have excelled in different areas of life – in physical development (even if you have some form of handicap), in educational accomplishments, in career, vocation, and relationships. Congratulations! Do not take your life for granted, as there are many out there who would wish to accomplish some of the things you have.

In my case, I struggled through the university as I had to enroll as a full-time student and worked full-time under some painful and difficult conditions. Through the ordeals, I hoped and never doubted that I would complete my studies. Looking back now, a number of external factors outside my control could have stopped me from getting through the university. But I have every reason to thank God that He prevailed for me. I remember how I always looked forward to graduation and joining the workforce. Upon completing my undergraduate program, I started to take my university accomplishment for granted. Two years later, I started my master's degree program, which would not have been possible without my undergraduate degree. The undergraduate degree created the platform upon which I was able to make further educational accomplishments. Our ability to overcome past challenges should give us the assurance and courage necessary to overcome current and future challenges. Past accomplishments provide platforms upon which future successes are built.

When God gave instructions through Moses to the Israelites, they heeded them, knowing that He was well capable of seeing to the fulfillment. When God puts a desire in you to do what appears to be impossible, because it is God putting it in there, be confident and run with it to completion. Be certain that you are hearing from God, and once convinced step into it! God has an impeccable track record for doing what people deem impossible. He knows the end from the beginning. He already has the plan mapped out when He inspires you to travel a path or initiate a cause or begin a venture. The Scriptures says: "it is God who works in you both to will and to do His good pleasure" (Philippians 2:13).

God calls you, sets you on the pathways to your destiny, and equips you to succeed. He gives you the grace required to complete the courses He sets you on and renders divine enablement to finish the projects He entrusts to you. Noah is an example you can draw inspiration from. There is no limit to what you can accomplish through God, except for self-imposed limits. If you need material resources, they all belong to God, "for the earth is the Lord's and all its fullness" (1 Corinthians 10:26). He can direct and/or redirect resources (tangible and intangible) to you at the right time and season, for the fulfillment of your destiny. He will work in you both to will and to do His good pleasure. Proverbs 21:1 says that "the king's heart is in the hand of the LORD, like the rivers of water; He turns it wherever He wishes."

The Wilderness

In Exodus 11:3, having just brought Moses, who was unknown, out of the wilderness, God caused Moses to be highly esteemed by the Israelites and the Egyptians alike. He had returned from a forty-year sojourn in the wilderness, where he had to learn full dependence on God and humility. He needed a significant shift from placing reliance on his position as a palace-bred kid who took matters into his own hands to dependence on God, who made it possible for him to be spared from Pharaoh's deadly decree in the first place. Imagine Moses, a prince in Egypt, on a freefall from the position of influence and prominence to being a fugitive and shepherd in the wilderness! But God pulled him back from that lowly state and placed him on a platform equal as it were to Pharaoh, who was seen as Egypt's god.

When you go through wilderness-type experiences of life, do not despair. God is still very much in control of your life. If you will yield to His instructions, your time and season of pulling out and up will certainly come and He will elevate you. He wants you to be great and will help establish you in the time of His choosing, as you walk with Him in obedience and humility.

In the same way it takes a child a series of developmental stages to reach full maturity, the actualization of our destinies takes time and comes in stages. Graduation through pertinent stages in life is imperative for destinies to be realized and optimized. Consequently, no stage in the development process can be skipped or rushed. However, delays in the developmental process can occur. In progressing through the stages of our destiny, it helps to know that completing a stage is prerequisite to beginning the next. Some stages are shorter than others, and some stages are more desirable than others.

The transitional stages in which you grow, develop, and prepare for the next stage are what I call "wildernesses." Wildernesses are usually undesirable. They can be likened to an institution of higher learning. Different institutions and courses have different learning objectives and varying levels of difficulty. Any real form of completion, progression, or graduation is determined by success at relevant tests. Success at the wilderness stages of our lives prepares us for progression and higher responsibilities or opportunities.

Wildernesses are painful but necessary places of transition in life. After being announced by John the Baptist to everyone at the river Jordan, and the Spirit of God having descended on Him, Jesus was led into the wilderness by the Spirit of God in order to be tested (prepared and made ready) for the commencement of His public ministry.

It was possible for Jesus' public ministry to have kicked off after being endorsed by a credible and influential John the Baptist, who came in the spirit of the prophet Elijah, followed by heavenly confirmation by the Holy Spirit in the form of a dove. Instead, the Holy Spirit in divine wisdom led Jesus to the wilderness to be tested, prepared, and made ready for ministry – toward the realization of His destiny.

You experience preparation and testing in your wilderness. It is nothing new. In any and all callings, including your career, your trade or education, you have to undergo wilderness seasons that prepare you for progression into higher responsibilities. Your season of preparation includes the formal or informal tests which, as you pass, advance you toward the next phase to fulfilling your destiny. Jesus repeatedly endured the hardship of the wilderness and passed the tests administered by Satan before advancing on His pathway to destiny.

When you go through experiences that some might refer to as "hell" watch out and stay steady. Just as it happened in the case of Jesus, whose public ministry gained tremendous traction right after the wilderness experience, wildernesses can be avenues for breakthrough and advancement.

We are given a full account of the commencement of Jesus' earthly ministry as prophesied by Isaiah (Luke 4:18-21). God's chosen time and season had come, and Jesus said "today this scrip-ture is fulfilled in your hearing" (Luke 4:21).

The wilderness is often a recurring transitional experience that we go through for a period of time preceding our progression to the next stage. In Hebrews 5:8 the Bible says of Jesus Christ that "though He was a Son, yet He learned obedience by the things which He suffered." Not only did Jesus go through the wilder-ness prior to His public ministry, He also went through the Garden of Gethsemane wilderness experience and several hard times in between. He did not avoid the wilderness, nor did He shy away from the cross. He yielded His will to God's will. God's will was for Jesus to experience the wilderness as He paid the ultimate price for mankind's sin by dying on the cross. He passed the test and fulfilled His purpose of coming to earth to save the human race and restoring us back to God. Having fulfilled His destiny, He was able to sit on the throne at the right hand of God – as if to teach us the popular slogan "no pain, no gain."

Also, an unsuccessful test-taker will often repeat the testing process if he fails at first attempt. To him, the wilderness experi-ence becomes recurring. He will have to go over the experience again, forego other pursuits, incur additional expenses, waste time, and make other sacrifices in order to prepare, pass the test, and then make progress.

Martin Luther was compelled to join the monastery where he was prepared and tested prior to confronting practices within the Roman Catholic Church of his day. The Roman Catholic Church was such a powerful institution at the time that it was dreaded by monarchies. Yet Martin Luther defied the fear of confrontation and its consequences and acted in what he believed God put in his heart to do by nailing the "ninety-five theses" on the doorposts of the Roman Catholic institution. At a time and season of God's choos-ing, while serving as a priest within the church, Martin Luther felt the prompting of God on his life to confront daunting issues in his day.

From the monastery (a form of wilderness) where much of his spiritual preparation occurred, Martin Luther advanced to become a Catholic priest, and while serving as a priest he was right in the heart of the issues he had been prepared to confront. Having been prepared he was able to understand and dispute "The Power and Efficacy of Indulgences" AKA "ninety-five theses." He was pushed again into the wilderness when he was excommunicated. But that ultimately advanced Martin Luther to becoming the "father of the Protestant Reformation."

Many never go on to fulfill their destinies because of fear of the wilderness; but those who choose God's path always fulfill their destiny – even if they die in the wilderness. Instances abound of many who went into their wilderness experiences trusting God that they would not die but live (Psalm 118:17), and they did not die! There were four notable outcasts with outstanding testimony of what God can do with anyone who will dare to go into his experience with faith and confidence in God. They were lepers and their story is told in 2 Kings 7:3-10. In Daniel 6 we read that Daniel did not succumb to fear and was thrown into the lions' den. God saved him and elevated Daniel.

After his encounter with Jesus on the way to Damascus, the apostle Paul, formerly known as Saul of Tarsus, was chosen by Jesus and sent to the wilderness where he was baptized and prepared by Ananias for the task to which he was called. At the time and season of God's choosing, great and effectual doors of ministry opened to Paul. Having progressed through the final wilderness, Paul admonished Timothy (his protégé) to "be diligent to present yourself approved to God, a worker who does not need to be ashamed, rightly dividing the word of truth" (2 Timothy 2:15).

Paul's counsel emanates from a wealth of life's wilderness experiences and embodies a fundamental principle for everyone on the path of calling or destiny. It applies to ministers, teachers, doctors, lawyers, accountants, engineers, contractors, etc. *You must be diligent to prove yourself worthy to be advanced on the day of your testing.* You will have to endure the various forms of wilderness-like experiences and excel at the tests that will come in the times and seasons that God has appointed for your advancement.

If you persevere in your wilderness experience, you will certainly advance as Jesus did, as Martin Luther did, as the four leprous men did, and as many others did before.

Changing Times and Seasons

On September 11, 2001, a terrorist attack was launched against the United States of America while George W. Bush Jr. was the president. That monumental event forced a shift in the president's policies, and he embarked on new policies pertaining to the war against terrorism. When he later ran for reelection, his handling of the terrorist attacks made him the ideal president for the nation, though the odds were stacked high against him. Key questions analysts hone into when a candidate runs to be elected or reelected to political office pertain to factors that helped in their election efforts such as policies, accomplishments, endorsements, etc. In the case of George Bush Jr., the majority of the American public was happy with his resolve, boldness, posture, and decisiveness against terrorism, and felt safer with him as president as opposed to his political rivals. His stance resonated with the wishes of most Americans in the times and seasons that the nation found herself.

Wilderness experiences, like what the United States under President Bush faced, always have profound ways of linking us with new paths that further the journey to our destinies. The times and seasons of wilderness are important in helping us hone our abilities and prepare us for successful advancement on the next phase of our destiny. An inspired wise man wrote that "I returned and saw under the sun that the race is not to the swift, nor the battle to the strong, nor bread to the wise, nor riches to men of understanding, nor favor to men of skill; but time and chance happen to them all" (Ecclesiastes 9:11).

In 2008, President Barack Obama took the American political landscape by storm. While he undoubtedly came across as a very bright and promising candidate, he ran against other bright and promising candidates with vast political experiences and endorsement of veteran politicians that far outweighed any chances Obama might have. Obama faced numerous challenges that included being a minority, having a Kenyan father, having ties with controversial pastor Jeremiah Wright, having an Arabic name (in an era of rising tensions due to terrorism by radical Islamists), and much more. Furthermore, Barack Obama was a newbie in the political arena. Interestingly, those same challenges that ordinarily would have worked against him seemed to work for him at the *time* of deep economic recession, and in a *season* of increased disdain for seasoned politicians, who were considered "more of the same."

To America, Obama represented hope and had a message and background as community organizer that gave him an undeniable platform for the race for presidency in a time and season of hope-lessness and despair. It was also a season in which globally people were poised for change from conventional qualities sought after in political leaders. It was in that season that Nicolas Sarkozy, a Frenchman of mixed national and ethnic ancestry, similar to Barack Obama, was elected as president of France.

Martin Luther, an iconic figure in the Protestant Reformation, was prepared in the wilderness as earlier mentioned but made tremendous impact in the church at a time and season in which change was imminent. It did not matter that the stakes were high and the mission critical; he was able to rise against the very power-ful Roman Catholic Church. Martin Luther emerged at a time of discontent with the abuse of power and gross misrepresentation of the truths contained in the Bible with the purpose of exploiting the people, who were mostly illiterate and ignorant of the bibli-cal truths. In those unprecedented times, Martin Luther, a Catholic priest, started a debate in the "ninety-five theses" that landed him on a new path to destiny that he had not previously imagined. With God-ordained circumstances outside of Martin Luther's control, he traveled a path that radically altered the Roman Catholic Church and birthed the Protestant church.

It is not coincidence that in that season initiatives were also being undertaken in other parts of Europe to bring about reformation. That era saw the rise of other prominent reformers such as John Calvin (France), Huldrych Zwingli (Switzerland), John Knox (Scotland), and others. By observing local and global trends and discerning how you fit in, you are better poised to seize destiny-making moments.

Destiny-making moments and events come with changing times and seasons that usually arrive unannounced. This was true for Martin Luther and many other great men and women who left massive footprints on earth. Martin Luther received his bachelor's and master's degrees and proceeded to enroll in law school – at his father's behest. That was to change by a thunderstorm in the summer of 1505, when a lightning bolt stuck near him on his way returning to the law school. The terrified Luther cried out, "Help, St. Anne! I'll become a monk!" – thinking that he was under some form of spell. His life was spared, but he regretted his promise to St. Anne. He kept his promise nonetheless even at the expense of his law school pursuit. He entered the monastery. Gleaning through his life, it is clear that he was being prepared all along for the Reformation, and with time and changing seasons he fulfilled his destiny.

Changing times and seasons play significant roles in the trajectory of our destinies. In times of economic depression/recession, for example, many people are forced to return to school, learn new skills, become entrepreneurs, pursue innovations, and ultimately position themselves for success.

Events outside our control with potential to direct or redirect our destiny pathway abound. They come without prior notice, but they come for our good and the benefit of others. It is helpful to recognize those events and to be ready to position ourselves to ride the tide and advance our life course, rather than becoming surprised and frightened. At such times, we need understanding and courage. We need to harness our capabilities, skills, and experiences and further preparations in order to advance and progress.

Without doubt, changing times and seasons present their peculiar challenges on the surface, but underneath them are silver linings of great opportunities for us to explore. We need to seize the moment and take on what seems impossible.

Like the children of Issachar in 1 Chronicles 12:32, who were well acquainted with times and seasons, we need to be aware of and understand the times and seasons so we can leverage our unique capabilities in the light of unfolding events and further our destinies. We need to discern when the "water of opportunity" is being troubled as was the case with the man at the pool of Bethesda (John 5:2-4) and prepare ourselves for a plunge at the right time – as we are led by the Spirit of God – in order to realize our breakthroughs. We need to respond appropriately when opportunity knocks.

It is not possible to know all things, but we should be able to connect the dots, make projections based on past events and trends, and draw inferences that will help us navigate the paths that present the most favorable outcome for our lives.

Moses, like Martin Luther, President Bush, President Obama, and others, did not have a clue how certain events would advance his destiny, but when changing times and seasons presented him with challenges, he saw opportunities that helped him prevail against all odds to realize his vision and move further along on the destiny journey. Imagine – the "I have a dream" speech (August 1963) by the much celebrated Rev. Martin Luther King Jr. came just a little over forty-four years prior to the realization, in the swearing in of America's forty-fourth president, Barack Obama (January 2008). That certainly could not have been a mere coincidence! The times, the season, and the context were right. Someone had the vision and another ran with it in due time and saw it become reality.

Times and seasons have repeatedly had significant implications in our life's journey. This book is an example of response to such turn of events. It was conceived at a time and season of my life while I was attending a theology class. A fellow student posed several questions pertaining to destiny: how we are to know what our destiny is; whether it is possible to miss one's destiny; could destiny be the product of hard work; do people just stumble on what later becomes their chance; is God biased in giving some what appears to be more favorable opportunities than others. As we reflected on these and other questions, the class struggled for answers that ended up inconclusive. In my mind, the contributions were ambiguous and further complicated the questions.

The next morning, as I was studying the book of Exodus, it was as if the light bulb came on in my mind and the answers came flooding in. There I was twelve hours later getting insight and revelation into destiny – outside of a theological class I would have thought should provide the answers. Beyond getting insight to the complex questions, I had a deep urge to write a book on the subject matter. The timing just seemed right. After praying about the subject matter, for which I sought answers for several years, I experienced a sudden prompting to write on the topic. This came only after I had sufficient life experience and insight into the Bible that God could utilize.

The answers that came in the process of writing this book did not come about all at once. What I had at the inception of this book project was a mere desire to write, coupled with an urge to discover answers pertaining to destiny.

74

Just as Moses had a number of unique experiences that stirred up the anger within him to do something—from his adoption into the Egyptian palace as a prince, to having an affectionate heart for his people, to his compassion for the Israelites and their plight in captivity under harsh slaving conditions, to his wilderness experience—I continued to have several events in my life that seemed to beg for my response to discover and write about the subject of DESTINY. Finally, the class situation brought it about, and I am grateful to God for the great joy and sense of fulfillment I have experienced in the course of this book project.

It is not possible to force the times and seasons of life as they are not in our control. We all have appointed times for specific tasks, accomplishments, and so on. Attempts to make things happen before their appointed times often lead to undesirable outcomes and frustration. That was Moses' experience when he took matters into his own hands and killed an Egyptian. We know of Moses' frustration because he named his first son Gershom, which means "*I have been a stranger in a foreign land*" (Exodus 2:22).

In God's appointed time and season, things began to fall into place for Moses. His flight from Egypt, his marriage to Zipporah the daughter of Jethro (priest of Midian), and his experience as a shepherd all helped propel him in the direction lined up for him by God. In the wilderness of his life, while growing, maturing, learning, and developing family ties, Moses was being prepared for what lay ahead in Egypt. When God's appointed four hundred years was up, and the perfect time and season came, Moses was fully ready as God's instrument to fulfill what he had known to be his God-given desires. In Exodus 2:24, the Bible says that God heard Israel's groaning and remembered His covenant.

God always hears us and never forgets His promises and covenants toward us. God answered the Israelites as can be seen in Exodus 2:25 because the appointed time to act had come. At the appointed time and season, following the death of the king of Egypt in Exodus 2:23, the lights came on and the Israelites realized their deplorable condition in bondage and cried to God. The preparation of Moses in the wilderness, the change of king in Egypt, and the discontent of the Israelites all converged at the right time for the fulfillment of God's promised deliverance after four hundred years.

Everything has its time and season, including the church Reformation under Luther and Zwingli, the abolition of slavery in America under President Abraham Lincoln (1865), and the swearing in of a person of color as America's forty-fourth president (2008).

Ecclesiastes 3 reassures us, "There is a <u>time</u> for everything, and a <u>season</u> for every activity under the heavens: a time to be born and a time to die, a time to plant and a time to uproot, a time to kill and a time to heal, a time to tear down and a time to build, a time to weep and a time to laugh, a time to mourn and a time to dance, a time to scatter stones and a time to gather them, a time to embrace and a time to refrain from embracing, a time to search and a time to give up, a time to keep and a time to throw away, a time to tear and a time to mend, a time to be silent and a time to speak, a time to love and a time to hate, a time for war and a time for peace. What do workers gain from their toil? I have seen the burden God has laid on the human race. He has made everything beautiful in its time. He has also set eternity in the human heart; yet no one can fathom what God has done from beginning to end."

Time is a resource that cannot be replenished. It comes and goes. Once gone, it cannot be retracted. Times and seasons are critical factors in our pathways to destiny. We cannot control times and seasons, but recognizing their changes, discerning how we fit in, and responding accordingly are crucial to fulfilling our destinies. Times and seasons, within and outside of life's wildernesses, serve tremendous purposes as we trek toward our God-given destiny. Appropriate understanding of both factors impacts our destiny and helps us better prepare for and seize opportunities when they unfold.

Your response to times and season:
1. Take a moment to reflect on and describe the time and season of life you are currently in. How do you fit in?

2. What wilderness season/experience are you currently undergoing? What opportunities are you uniquely positioned to capitalize on?

3. What lessons are you learning in order to prepare for the test to follow?

4. What season do you perceive God is preparing you for next?
    a. How are you preparing?
    b. How receptive are you to learning obedience, as Jesus did?
    c. How courageous are you?

Chapter Seven:

Revelation

"But as it is written: "Eye has not seen, nor ear heard, nor have entered into the heart of man the things which God has prepared for those who love Him."
– 1 Corinthians 2:9.

"Everyone has a destiny; you just have to discover it."
– Osamede Ogbomo

God has plans and purposes for each of His creations, and there is a book written specifically about each of us. More often than not, those things are never fully known by us up front, except in the case of Jesus Christ. In His case, Jesus knew what was written concerning Him and He went about from the onset to fulfill God's plan and purpose (Hebrews 10:5-9). To us, however, there are many of God's plans and purposes relating to our destiny that we do not quite know except through revelation. Divine revelation, divine guidance, and divine provision are interrelated mediums through which God enables us to realize our destiny.

Divine Revelation

Every major invention and accomplishment is born out of revelation, which makes revelation a very important factor in the destiny mix. In order to fulfill our destiny, it is important to seek God for revelation as well as clarity/understanding of what is revealed.

Divine revelation involves getting insight, through supernatural help, into something that is already in existence but which till then has been concealed. It is the grace to see solutions to problems.

The solutions are already there but waiting to be discovered. While problems abound on earth, God has already given us the solutions. Every unsolved problem is simply waiting for the solution to be discovered (revealed).

The Bible is replete with narratives of great accomplishments and transformations through divine revelation. Noah built an ark and preserved the human race as a result of divine revelation (Genesis 6-8). Abraham came out of pagan practice and began a journey that would impact every generation after him through divine revelation and guidance. Without divine provision and revelation of the substitute for his son in Genesis 22:13, this father of faith could have innocently killed his son Isaac at Mount Moriah. In Genesis 22:8 we read about Abraham making a declaration of faith that God will provide: "God himself will provide the lamb for the burnt offering..." – an all-important declaration toward fulfilling destiny. He saw God make propitiation for his son at the time in Moriah, while also pointing to Calvary.

You wonder where the ram came from and why Abraham did not previously see it. Also, what caused Abraham to lift up his eyes to see the provision behind him in the nick of time? Abraham would not have seen the ram if his attention was not called to it by divine revelation through the angel of the Lord (Genesis 22:11), or if he failed to respond in obedience to the revelation when his attention was drawn to it (Genesis 22:13).

Hagar conceived for Abraham and through revelation knew that Ishmael's destiny would be great (Genesis 16:10-12). By revelation, Hagar preserved the life of Ishmael (Genesis 21:15-19).

Moses led an entire nation out of bondage by revelation (Exodus 3:2-10) and received revelations throughout the exodus ordeal on what he needed to do to further their journey to the Promised Land. Several more instances of people being guided to destiny by divine revelation abound throughout the Bible.

Divine Guidance

Divine guidance, divine revelation, and divine provision go together. While divine revelation enables us to obtain supernatural perception (or reality) of what is in existence, or what will be, so as to know what to do at certain times in order to get specific results, divine guidance on the other hand pertains to supernatural direction on steps to take, decisions to make, and/or paths to follow. As you go about life, you are bound to encounter challenges. It is your responsibility to ask God for both revelation and guidance in order to overcome and continue onward toward fulfilling your destiny. When you become unsure of what to do, cry out to God in prayer as Moses and several other faith-worthies did.

Several times on their way to the Promised Land, Moses and his people cried to God when they met with difficulties or were perplexed and did not know what to do next. In Exodus 14:15, for instance, God told Moses: "why are you crying to me? Tell the children of Israel to go forward...." That was divine guidance! There is a time to cry and a time to act. As if to further give specifics on how to go forward, God said to Moses: "...lift up your rod, and stretch out your hand over the sea and divide it. And the children of Israel shall go on dry ground through the midst of the sea" (Exodus 14:16). Here was a perfect mix of divine guidance and divine revelation at work.

Divine guidance can be derived in the form of visions, dreams, gut feelings, intuition, hunches, or some other miraculous intervention. There are some overlaps since you get divine revelation in similar ways. While divine revelation and knowledge is insight gained from God on what is, or what will be, divine guidance involves being supernaturally led on what to do. "Informed" guesses may produce desired results from time to time but cannot be guaranteed or relied upon unless God's hands are on them. That is the reason we all need to have God ordering our steps.

Proverbs 16:9 says that *"A man's heart plans his way, but the* Lord *directs his steps."* The best minds in investment management circles or the best mathematical models used for investment decisions fail. Hence investors are often advised that past performance is not indicative or a guarantee of future results. Only God can guarantee and deliver on His promises. You receive from God by divine providence, gain insight by divine revelation, and enter into fulfillment by divine guidance.

In Exodus 13:17-22 God began to lead the Israelites with specific instructions on the path they were to follow. This guidance was chosen by God for Israel with absolute foreknowledge and the best of intentions. In order to succeed, the Israelites needed to wholly depend on God.

Obedience

Obedience to God helps make our journey easier, less stressful, and successful while disobedience is most often the precursor to failure. While it is quite rewarding, obedience can be challenging. If you choose to obey God and let Him guide your steps, you stand to benefit greatly from Him. To obey God begins by learning about His commandments and His ways. When the leadership baton was passed from Moses to Joshua and he was preparing to lead the Israelites to their ultimate prophetic and geographic destination in the exodus journey, they were told: "This Book of the Law shall not depart from your mouth, but you shall meditate in it day and night, that you may observe to do according to all that is written in it. For then you will make your way prosperous, and then you will have good success" (Joshua 1:8).

There is often the temptation to take the short route or follow the crowd. It is natural to want to get desired results quickly by taking the shortest route possible. Avoid this temptation. Determine to stick with God's supernatural plans and directions, even when the ideal pathway for you appears longer and the journey seems to take more time. God took the Israelites through a longer path (the sea) on their way to Canaan because He had an exhilarating adventure of a lifetime and miracle in mind that would forever stop the Egyptians from chasing after them.

You would make steady progress through the ranks and shorten the distance and time by learning obedience and growing in your faith in God. In addition to the adventure and miracle of parting the Red Sea, God led the Israelites through the wilderness for forty years on a journey that should have taken eleven days! The choice is yours to develop obedience to God and faith in Him and let Him guide you to fulfilling your destiny at the time and season of His choosing. Of course you may choose to go your way and spend your lifetime doing what should have taken you a relatively short time to accomplish.

Obedience and faith are invaluable in our walk with God. God administers tests of our obedience at different stages of life. Unlike the prescheduled tests taken in the course of formal education, God's tests are usually unannounced. You never know when the next test will be given, so you ought to be prepared at all times by getting your heart right with God. When your test is handed over to you, the condition of your heart will determine your performance. God often tests ahead of promotion to see if we will obey and to assess our worthiness and preparedness for elevation. He does not grade on the curve either, as His standards are set.

David was obedient to God and fulfilled his destiny (1 Kings 14:8). Saul on the other hand was disobedient and aborted God's plans for his life (1 Samuel 15:11-26). Gideon, like the other judges of Israel, excelled when he obeyed God (Judges 7) but disintegrated when he disobeyed (Judges 8:24-27). Obedience can be painful yet rewarding. Jesus "learned obedience by the things which He suffered" (Hebrews 5:8) and went on to fulfill His destiny. Adam, by contrast, disobeyed God and destroyed his destiny. God is clear about what He expects from you. Like Ezra, you need to decide in your heart to seek out His laws and to do them. "Ezra had prepared his heart to seek the law of the LORD, and to do it, and to teach statutes and ordinances in Israel" (Ezra 7:10). Ignorance of God's law is no defense and can be quite expensive.

Revelation in Moses' Journey

God was teaching Moses and all Israel a serious lesson on divine revelations. In Exodus 7:1, for instance, God compelled a brutal and arrogant ruler that saw himself as god to perceive Moses with great regard – as god. Imagine also that Aaron, the elder brother to Moses, deferred to his younger brother in spite of the fact that the prevailing culture placed a premium on seniority and chronology. Note also that in that same passage (Exodus 7:1) God told Moses to "see." Divine revelation involves seeing. Your ability to see what God sees beyond your ordinary physical ability is very valuable.

Many people have varying degrees of limited vision. Many have no clue where they are headed in the journey of life. Some go in and out of short-lived dreams and never make any significant inroads because the threats posed by destiny killers outweigh their limited vision. Vision is powered by revelation, which requires faith to become reality; and faith is opposed to all forms of destiny killers including fear, doubt, and discouragement.

Perhaps God has given you an express mission and assignment, or placed a desire in your heart to venture into something bigger than you can seemingly wrap your arms around. Rest assured that if God is in it, you either already have what it takes to succeed or those things have been divinely provided for, even though they may not be so obvious yet. You may encounter some daunting challenges along the way. You are not immune to challenges. If you are faithful and obedient, you will certainly succeed. You need the ability to see clearly and to obey what has been revealed in order to embark on and accomplish big dreams.

What God prompted Moses to "see" happening with Pharaoh and Aaron were beyond his physical and mental abilities. God wanted Moses to see a new reality as a result of a shift in the spiritual realm. Moses had a newfound revelation and understanding of a reality that his natural senses could not comprehend. God was at work and wanted Moses to see that he had made Moses a god to Pharaoh. Moses was no longer the man who fled Egypt for his life, but rather a new man whose paths had been prepared by God. He was now in a new season of life and needed to come to terms with that reality in order to optimize his potential. When Moses began to do what God called him to do in his interaction with Pharaoh, his past was never brought up. It was a new day! Instead, Pharaoh looked to Moses in high regard and never ordered his servants to seize Moses or to harm him in any way.

Pharaoh undoubtedly saw Moses as a threat to his kingdom but could not eliminate him. Moses became a new man, a new creation, with a new identity. If you are in Christ, you are a renewed and transformed person with no limitations along the destiny paths God has laid out for you. Like Moses, you need to "see" your new reality and embrace it. The Bible tells us in 2 Corinthians 5:17 "if anyone is in Christ, he is a new creation; old things have passed away; behold, all things have become new." Our new reality is guaranteed by the finished work at Calvary; Jesus fully paid for our redemption and transformation (Hebrews 10:16-20).

To fulfill your destiny, you need to see yourself as God sees you, as opposed to the limited physical perspective you are accustomed to. As you see your new state and reality, be careful to discern God's provisions for you as well. You have everything you need to succeed in the race of life. Don't wait till you see everything. Set out by faith from where you are today because "he who observes the wind will not sow, and he who regards the clouds will not reap" (Ecclesiastes 11:4). You cannot allow the things you see today, including the limitations, inabilities, and disabilities, to dictate the trajectory of your life; have faith in God because "without faith it is impossible to please Him" (Hebrews 11:4).

Resist the urge to view things from a limited perspective, as that would undermine your ability to achieve your destiny. Do not focus on limitations in your talents, resources, connections, or experiences, as they have the potential to paralyze you. Instead, pray that God will help you see things from His undistorted perspective. It is He who predestined you and makes all things work together for your good. If you travel the paths God has ordained for you without violating His rules, He will ensure that you succeed.

View the calling of God on your life as a project, with Him as the project owner, whose vested interest is always protected – for your success and His glory. See as God sees. That was what Moses did. Even though he could not tell what challenges lay ahead of him in the wilderness, or the enormity of provision that would be required to survive in the wilderness, he was nonetheless convinced that the Almighty God had everything covered. He did! Moses just had to walk by faith daily.

As Moses received "progressive" revelations of God's provision, he became increasingly courageous to step out of his comfort zone and do what God was asking him to do from stage to stage. God gave Aaron as a resource to Moses as he approached Pharaoh. He also gave Him the rod as well as supernatural power for confirmation (Exodus 4:1-17). God revealed to Moses that He had already paved the way for him to stand before Pharaoh and other challenges that may confront him. Revelation is a critical factor to success.

Self-awareness

Divine revelation begins with knowing who you are and is necessary to optimize your potential. John the Baptist excelled in his calling for as long as he knew who he was in relation to the Messiah. When asked who he was, he was quick to point out: "'I am not the Christ'…'I am the voice of one calling in the desert, Make straight the way for the Lord'" (John 1:19-27). He was just the forerunner, the messenger. There was One coming after him, Jesus Christ, the only begotten Son of the living God, whose sandals he was not worthy to untie. You must know who you are without pretensions because you cannot excel trying to fit in someone else's shoes.

You cannot truly know who you are until you first know who God is. It is God that gives you proper revelation of who you are. The more you know of God, the more you discover yourself and the more you are able to hear Him and partake in what He is saying and doing. Embrace your true identity in Christ; act by faith on what God is saying to you and showing you, and be a part of what He is doing in the world.

Divine Providence

As Israel went through the wilderness, God made sure they had what they needed for sustenance. For example, in Exodus 15:27 we read: "they came to Elim, where there were twelve springs of water and seventy palm trees; so they camped there by the waters." Not only were the numbers of significance, but the findings speak of God's supernatural providence for those He leads. We see God's supernatural provision throughout the journey to the Promised Land and throughout the Scriptures at large. The sojourners must have imagined who dug those wells and whether there was a city and people there before. Why would a choice place with flourishing wells and suitable vegetation, as indicated by the palm trees, be deserted? God led the Israelites to *still waters* and *green pastures* as the psalmist describes in Psalm 23:2. God will always lead you to places of rest and comfort. He is the Good Shepherd who will always care for and provide for you.

The number twelve represents the sons of Jacob, or the totality of the people of Israel that God brought out of captivity. The seventy palm trees represent prosperity, fruitfulness, shelter, good habitation, and fertility. Those trees also symbolized the rest of the Gentiles. It is comforting to know that beyond the Jews, God has made provision for non-Jews (Gentiles) that will turn to spiritual Israel through the knowledge of Him.

We experience supernatural provision in various forms throughout our life's journey. There are times when we have no worries in the pathways of our destiny and are flourishing in our careers, businesses, ministries, etc. At such times, it is tempting to dwell at those spots and become complacent. But while we enjoy the momentary spots while they last, we must be prepared to get up and continue on to fulfilling our destiny. Elim was not Israel's destination, so they needed to enjoy it for the duration they were appointed to linger there, but eventually move forward.

Discernment

On the course toward fulfilling your destiny, you will be presented with different ideas and interests. You will hear multiple voices (audible and inaudible) and arrive at junctions with divergent pathways. Amidst all the confusion and perplexities is that dire need for discernment. Without discernment, you are prone to making costly mistakes that will undermine your ability to fulfill your destiny. Discernment is an essential quality we all need to fulfill our destiny. ("...this I pray, that your love may abound still more and more in knowledge and all discernment..." Philippians 1:9); "...cry out for discernment, and lift up your voice for understanding" Proverbs 2:3) This is especially true as people are increasingly faced with the threat of being displaced by all sorts of doctrines and ideologies that seem credible to the mind but are contrary to the true Word of God and therefore destructive. The days that the apostle Peter prophesied in his epistle (2 Peter 2:1) when false teachers will deny the Lord, propagate heresies, and bring damnation are here. Jesus Christ also warned us against "ravening wolves" (Matthew 7:15). There are all kinds of nicely packaged New Age and strange religious concepts, and it is our duty to discern the truth from falsehood.

We cannot but heed the apostle Paul's repeated exhortation to those who would follow Christ: "Brethren, join in following my example, and note those who so walk, as you have us for a pattern. For many walk, of whom I have told you often, and now tell you even weeping, that they are the enemies of the cross of Christ" (Philippians 3:17-18). Jesus said: "My sheep hear My voice, and I know them, and they follow Me" (John 10:27).

Spiritual discernment means hearing what God has to say and following Him where He leads. In order to discern counsel that contradicts the will of God for your life, you need to know God for yourself. You need points of reference that come from diligently meditating on God's Word: hearing and learning from God. You won't know if the spiritual leaders you are following are genuine followers of Christ or not if you do not know Christ for yourself and if God's Word doesn't "dwell in you richly" (Colossians 3:16).

When we were babies, we believed everything our parents told us because we did not have the faculty, intelligence, and experience to know otherwise for ourselves. As we grew into maturity and accumulated knowledge and experience, we were no longer as gullible. Rather, we were able to question some of the things we were taught and discern things that are untrue. We could only do this because we developed. Joshua 1:8 says that "This Book of the Law shall not depart from your mouth, but you shall meditate in it day and night, that you may observe to do according to all that is written in it. For then you will make your way prosperous, and then you will have good success" (Joshua 1:8).

Communion with God has become increasingly challenging as we advance technologically, being bombarded with information and misinformation and exposed to various forms of garbage and distraction. Consequently, it requires diligent discernment to separate the grain from the chaff and incline our hearts and ears to the true Word of God. He speaks to us if we choose to listen. He speaks in a still small voice – often. We are best positioned to hear God in the place of quietness. He also speaks through our parents, spouses, children, and godly ministers. God says: "Be still, and know that I am God; I will be exalted among the nations, I will be exalted in the earth!" (Psalm 46:10). Irrespective of whom we perceive that God speaks through or how, the words that we receive should never contradict the Word or nature of God.

For example, Sarai advised Abram to take her maidservant, Hagar, for his wife (Genesis 16:3) in order to help God bring about the fulfillment of God's previous promise to him (Genesis 15:4). While Sarai had good intentions, her scheme was contrary to the nature of God, who ordained that marriage would be comprised of one man and one woman from the beginning. By introducing another woman into the equation, they were working against God's plan and disrupting the balance of a healthy marriage. Besides, God does not require the help or manipulation of man to bring about His plan. When Sarai later motioned to send Hagar packing (Genesis

21:10), God told Abraham to listen to his wife. That is true discernment. I believe God's position on the matter was a reflection of His will then and now, and allowed for the restoration of balance and harmony in the home.

As God's children, we should grow in knowledge of Him and get to a place whereby the counsel we receive from others is confirmation of what God has already said to us or clearly prepared us for. If, as God's children with a basic understanding of His ways, we're told to do something absurd or unsettling, great caution should be exercised.

In 1 Kings 13 is a sad story of a man of God from Judah who was walking the path of his calling during the reign of King Jeroboam. The king tried to entice the prophet by inviting him to his house and offering him a reward. "But the man of God said to the king, if you were to give me half your house, I would not go in with you; nor would I eat bread nor drink water in this place. For so it was commanded me by the word of the LORD, saying, 'You shall not eat bread, nor drink water, nor return by the same way you came'" (1 Kings 13:8-9). At this point, the prophet discerned aright. He knew what was expected of him by God and was ready to stand firm on what God said as opposed to what the king entreated.

Being human, the same prophet was later deceived by another old prophet who "…said to him, 'I too am a prophet as you are, and an angel spoke to me by the word of the LORD, saying, bring him back with you to your house, that he may eat bread and drink water.' (He was lying to him). So he went back with him, and ate bread in his house, and drank water. Now it happened, as they sat at the table, that the word of the LORD came to the prophet who had brought him back; and he cried out to the man of God who came from Judah, saying, 'Thus says the LORD: "Because you have disobeyed the word of the LORD, and have not kept the commandment which the LORD your God commanded you, but you came back, ate bread, and drank water in the place of which the LORD said to you, 'Eat no bread and drink no water,' your corpse shall not come to the tomb of your fathers." So it was, after he had eaten bread and after he had drunk, that he saddled the donkey for him, the prophet whom he had brought back. When he was gone, a lion met him on the road and killed him. And his corpse was thrown on the road, and the donkey stood by it. The lion also stood by the corpse" (1 Kings 13:18-24).

What a story of poor discernment and a good lesson to warn each of us of the need for proper discernment. He believed and acted upon what the old prophet said (which was contrary to what God told him), supposing that he was a true prophet. But the old prophet, like every false, deceitful minister (2 Corinthians 11:13-15), acted as an angel of light and caused the steps of the younger prophet to be derailed and his destiny destroyed. We must be extra careful to know what God is saying in order to fulfill our destiny. Anything that runs contrary to God's will for our lives will always lead to derailment and failure.

When Jethro counseled Moses to establish an effective leadership structure, he said to Moses, "'If you do this thing, and God so commands you, then you will be able to endure, and all this people will also go to their place in peace.' So Moses heeded the voice of his father-in-law and did all that he had said" (Exodus 23-24) because he was convinced that God commanded him so. Jethro, by wisdom, was mindful that Moses needed to seek God's approval when he counseled: "If you do this thing, and God so commands you...." Men's counsel, no matter how plausible and credible, must at all times align with God's will for our lives or we could be treading the path of abortive destiny.

Chapter questions:
1. How is your spiritual vision (ability to see beyond the ordinary)? If dull, pray for revelation.

2. Is God your primary guide when making major decisions, or do you mainly trust in yourself and others? Proverbs 3:5 says that you should "trust in the Lord with all your heart, and lean not on your understanding".

3. Have you overstayed your welcome in your present station in life? Ask God for revelation of the next phase, and for divine guidance.

Chapter Eight:

Divine Appointment

"But rise and stand on your feet; for I have appeared to you for this purpose, to make you a minister and a witness both of the things which you have seen and of the things which I will yet reveal to you."
– Acts 26:16

"There is no such thing as chance; and what seem to us merest accidents spring from the deepest source of destiny."
– Johann Friedrich Von Schiller

Throughout history people are born, divinely appointed, and raised up to accomplish specific purposes in life. There is a direct link between events in the lives of people, the situations they are born into, and the purpose they are called to fulfill. When divine appointments are fulfilled, history is made that transcends generations. Good examples include John the Baptist, who was Jesus' forerunner and under whose ministry the practice of baptism was established; the Lord Jesus Christ (though God He came to earth as a man) who birthed Christianity that continues to endure into eternity; Pope Gregory and the Roman Catholic Church reformations that remain in effect today; and Martin Luther, the father of Protestantism, whose work continues to be celebrated.

It may not always be clear-cut what our appointment in life is. Fortunately, there are clues along life's pathways that may help unravel our appointed destinies, or at least the next phase. In the life of Moses, for example, it was not sufficiently clear what his calling or destiny was. He made a few missteps that facilitated his wilderness experience. Trapped in the extremities of two worlds, Moses the adopted Egyptian prince had enviable powers and privileges, while being pulled by innate compassion for the sufferings of the Hebrew people with whom he identified in Egypt. There seemed to be a strong pull between these paradoxical worlds. He could perhaps not understand why he ended up in the wilderness as shepherd over Jethro's animals.

We are often caught up in the complexities of life and do not always know why we are in the situations we find ourselves in, what precise decisions to make, where we should be, which way to go, and how to go about it. We often lack clarity on what constitutes appropriate response to changing times and seasons that are evident in life events. We could console ourselves by knowing this problem isn't peculiar to us, as it has been so from time past. Moses and several other success stories had to deal with the same issues.

Back to Moses' life journey: he traveled a path that brought him in the company of two of his Hebrew compatriots who were involved in a fight. Being unclear of his destiny, as it pertained to the liberation of Israel, he attempted to broker peace between the two Hebrews, only to be rebuffed with "who made you prince and judge over us?" Clue! Prince and judge! What a clue and pointer to his divine appointment: prince (leader) and judge (custodian of God's law). He became both at God's appointed time. The two fighting Hebrew men were Moses' incidental witnesses, providing him the clue of who God was calling him to become, just as was the case with Samuel, who became incidental witness to both Saul and David – future kings of Israel.

Another clue that pointed to Moses' destiny was his compelling instinctive *yearning* to stand up for the Hebrews. He was constantly stirred up from within to intervene in matters relating to his people, the Hebrews. Twice he attempted in his human effort to "fight for" his fellow citizens, but those were well ahead of God's timing. The passion to do something was so compelling that Moses was not mindful of the riches and glamour of the Egyptian palace. As far as he was concerned, being a prince of Egypt was not it. He felt, and rightly so, that there was more to his life, more to his purpose, and more to his destiny than enjoying the pleasures of the Egyptian palace. He was zealous for his people; he felt their *pain* and shared their cry for justice and freedom. Those were strong clues that helped Moses to stay on the right path of service – his inner yearning and unfolding events.

Understanding this point helps us in our quest to discover our pathways to destiny.

To discover destiny, it is important that we step aside to ask ourselves the question: what would I do if I had the power and resources to change situations and circumstances? What is my heart's cry? What am I drawn to? What issues in my local or global community do I feel compelled to bring solutions to? Mahatma Gandhi, Martin Luther King Jr., Mother Teresa, and a host of others are examples of great leaders that felt the pain of the people they were called to serve. They left their comfort zones and stood against unprecedented circumstances to defend the weak and fight for justice, and inadvertently fulfilled their destinies and left legacies behind that transcended their generations. Their yearnings led them to seize great opportunities (in what an average person would deem "lost causes") to fulfill their destinies as they made significant impact in the lives of others.

Divine appointment compelled Moses' mother, among several other Hebrew mothers in Egypt, to build a "floating ark" for her child while others chose either to do nothing or perhaps shy away from the situation. Divine appointment brought Pharaoh's daughter at the very same time and place on the Nile River to discover the "goodly child," adopt him, and to accept Moses' mother (unknown to the princess) to care for the baby at the recommendation of the baby's sister, also unknown to the princess. Perfect arrangement and divine appointment!

These weren't coincidences in light of the bigger picture. God was connecting the dots and putting the pieces of the complex puzzle in place: the Hebrew midwives, Moses' mother's intuition, Miriam's counselor role, Pharaoh's daughter... God was certainly ordering the paths of the different stakeholders in extraordinary ways in order to fulfill Moses' individual destiny and the Hebrews' corporate destiny.

In 1 Samuel 17 is the story of David's confrontation with Goliath after he became aroused in anger against the Philistine's defiance of Israel's army. By divine appointment, God arranged the meeting, stirred up David's emotions, and helped him prevail against Goliath - the Philistine champion.

Divine appointment and inspiration manifests in different forms, as we can deduce from the stories of Moses and David. It manifests in the life of anyone who will accomplish some great things for God and for the greater good of mankind. In life, we find ourselves getting connected with people and circumstances in ways we find difficult to explain. No event occurs by chance, and there are really no coincidences when it comes to destiny. Everything happens for a reason, so pay close attention to life events.

It takes wisdom to understand the times and seasons, like the children of Issachar (1 Chronicles 12:32). Pay attention to the times and seasons you are in, and take stock of your unique capabilities, passions, experiences, and talents in order to identify and seize opportunities and momentum in the right direction. We may not have the full picture of the outcome from the onset, but we should be aware internally and externally of clues.

Understanding of divine appointments in the context of the times and seasons in which Moses and David (and many others) found themselves, in spite of several mitigating factors, helped them make necessary shifts from the status quo. When we know our divine appointments in changing times and seasons, we are better positioned for change rather than get overwhelmed in the pathways to our destiny. Jethro's visit to Moses and the Israelites in the wilderness could be trivialized as a mere visit from a father in-law but is an example of divine appointment. Jethro observed Moses burning his candle at both ends in the process of managing his people. Jethro was positioned to call him aside and recommend the management concept of appointing hierarchical rulers/judges to whom Moses could delegate authority to lead the growing population (Exodus 18:1-26).

Continue to pay attention to the changing times and seasons and respond accordingly, as nothing ever remains constant. We must be ready to increase our capacity by delegating responsibilities and giving developmental opportunities to trustworthy individuals. To further our destiny and optimize our potential in life, we must endeavor to keep our eyes on the big picture rather than get bogged down with small details festered by self-centeredness. We must respond to changes in order to stay on the right course and advance on our destiny pathways.

Jethro understood the changing needs of the people and counseled Moses accordingly. Moses' relationship with Jethro, the timing of Jethro's visit, and his corresponding counsel were entirely by divine appointment. It was divine appointment that brought everything together to help advance Moses' destiny. Divine appointment will help you advance your destiny as well.

Destiny-making Moments

We encounter diverse people and circumstances at different stations in life. Some encounters are far more significant than others. My aforementioned experience in a classroom happened by divine appointment and proved to be a destiny-making moment that served as catalyst for another phase in my life journey. It was by divine appointment that the discussion occurred at a time when I was about to once again read through the book of Exodus in the Bible. Though I had read Exodus before, this time the light came on in my mind and I started to get insight on the subject of destiny from studying the life of Moses. I could then discern that there are combinations of factors that converge to help us fulfill our destinies.

Surprisingly, I developed a deep yearning to commence a book on how to discover one's destiny, even though my usual propensity in the past would be to take down sermon notes. I was convinced that as I embarked on this project, the Spirit of God would lead me into more truths and help unfold mysteries around the subject matter.

My starting point on the pathway to discovering destiny is that I saw a clear link between Moses' destiny and God's promise to lead the Israelites out of Egypt after staying under bondage for four hundred years. Not only did God inform Abraham that his descendants would be captives in Egypt, He promised to liberate them from captivity (Genesis 15:13). The divine revelation and promise of deliverance four hundred years earlier, followed by the convergence of the birth of Moses, his miraculous rescue, and upbringing in the Egyptian palace all bore witness to the validity of divine appointment. Moses, like everyone else, was sent here on earth for a mission. Put another way, Moses had a destiny to fulfill. As you study the take a closer look into the life of Moses, it becomes clear that he was being uniquely positioned to accomplish God's plan all along by divine appointment!

Also notice how God had told Abraham in Genesis 15:16 that "in the <u>fourth generation</u> your descendants will come back here." After Abraham, the first generation was the generation of Isaac; the second was that of Jacob; the third, Joseph; and the fourth generation, Moses. How precise! Notice that until Moses' generation came to the scene, the people seemed comfortable and had no reason for an exodus. However, the events and circumstances orchestrated by divine appointment would later compel them to move toward the fulfillment of their collective destiny, as promised by God. "Let God be true and every man a liar" (Romans 3:4, excerpt).

The new king of Egypt, Pharaoh, issued a command to the midwives to kill the boys and let the girls live (Exodus 1:15–17). This move was rather counterintuitive since the boys were more suited to be laborers than their female counterparts. By killing the boys when they were born, it was inevitable that Egypt would have a smaller supply of laborers in the future. A rational approach from a strategic standpoint would have been to spare the Hebrew boys and let them serve as domestic helpers and builders, while Egyptian boys were used for military purposes, thereby preserving the military might while building and maintaining the economic and internal infrastructure of Egypt.

Rather illogically, Pharaoh wanted all Hebrew boys dead. His reason was ridiculous, irrational, biased, and skewed: "Now there arose a new king over Egypt, who did not know Joseph. And he said to his people, 'Look, the people of the children of Israel are more and mightier than we; come, let us deal shrewdly with them, lest they multiply, and it happen, in the event of war, that they also join our enemies and fight against us, and so go up out of the land'"(Exodus 1:8-10). Similarly, at the time of Jesus' birth, Herod (of the same lineage as Pharaoh) was told by his diviners, astrologers, and magicians that a deliverer would be born King of the Jews. You could only imagine Herod's rage, fear, and jealousy leading to the order to kill the male Hebrew children two years and under (see Matthew 2:1-18).

Destiny-making moments are always the focus of strong oppositions – oppositions that are determined to thwart, and where possible, nullify destiny. Believers have a stronger assurance of divine protection in the face of such oppositions. Unknown to Herod and to Pharaoh, God had made promises concerning Jesus Christ and Moses that He would surely bring about – irrespective of the gates of hell that may stand in opposition.

On our pathways to destiny, we are often confronted by principalities, powers, and wickedness in high places; we need not be afraid or shy away. Rather, we should stand tall and keep our heads high, realizing that He who called us will see to it that we fulfill our destiny. God's assurance is: "...do not fear those who kill the body but cannot kill the soul. But rather fear Him who is able to destroy both soul and body in hell. Are not two sparrows sold for a copper coin? And not one of them falls to the ground apart from your Father's will. But the very hairs of your head are all numbered. Do not fear therefore; you are of more value than many sparrows" (Matthew 10:28-31). Seasons like these are signals we should embrace, pray against, and be confident to act in.

The September 11, 2001, terrorist attack on the United States of America is an example of divine appointment at work. It was a season of terror in America and throughout the Western world that required a U.S. president with the necessary resolve to handle the grim situation. The handling of that event helped shape the reelection of President George W. Bush Jr. Prior to the attack, President Bush seemed likely to lose a second term, as his approval was dwindling and he did not seem to have the confidence of the majority of Americans. Faced with a tough situation with overreaching implications, President Bush chose courage over fear. He chose the difficult path of confronting terrorism with the resolve shared widely by the majority of Americans including the military. That act of courage and resolve contributed in no small measure to his reelection.

Our unique capabilities and responses in difficult situations are critical destiny-making factors. We must be careful not to lose those unique God-given attributes as we look for and embrace various self-improvement initiatives. At the appointed times, when the conditions are right and the opportunities are present, the necessary connections between our unique attributes will converge with the times and seasons to make lasting impacts.

Bush undoubtedly had the desire to be reelected, and events beyond his control created a context whereby his desire and unique attributes as a person positioned him for reelection. His peculiar inherent attributes in connection with the peculiar events in the United States, which were beyond his control, propelled him further toward fulfilling his destiny. He had been preparing all his life, consciously or unconsciously, and when events occurred by divine appointment, he responded precisely in ways only he could have.

Boldness in the Face of Adversity: The Hebrew Midwives

The Hebrew midwives, though slaves themselves, feared God and did not heed Pharaoh's command to kill Hebrew sons (Exodus 1:15-17). This strategy should not be strange to anyone desiring to fulfill his destiny: Hebrew midwives called to kill Hebrew sons – their own! It is always true that powers of opposition will use your own people—familiar faces, possibly friends, family, and acquaintances—to infiltrate your camp in the bid to undo you and to frustrate God's will and purpose concerning you. Be bold and courageous. You have the everlasting arms around you (see Deuteronomy 33:27).

Thank God for people who choose not to be used by opposition to frustrate the success of their own people! Thank God for the Hebrew midwives. We read that God rewarded them for their decision not to kill the Hebrew sons (Exodus 1:21). The fact that the midwives "feared God" suggests a commitment to the revealed will of God, accompanied by reverence for and unshakable faith in the Almighty.

Jesus' disciples in Acts 4:1-3, 17-21, 31 were similarly emboldened by the Holy Spirit to preach the gospel of Jesus Christ though their lives were in danger, having been threatened by the rulers, elders, and scribes not to preach the gospel.

The first minority U.S. president had a lot working against him and could have chosen to focus on the negatives, or try as hard as he could to want to change them. He could have used them as excuses to stay off the pathway to the presidency. He chose instead a narrow and difficult path traveled by a few that would attempt greatness. Coupled with the fact that he had youthful zeal, fresh insights, and a message of hope, he was poised to take his world by storm. He did.

Most would find it incongruous for a Harvard University law graduate, with opportunity to work for a prestigious law firm, to abandon the niceties of his position for the slums of Chicago as a community organizer. But that was what Barack Obama did. Like Moses, he left beauty for ashes, gain for pain, and the comfort of finer life for the streets of Chicago to help the underprivileged. That was not a conventional track to the presidency, in the same way that being a shepherd boy was not a conventional track for David and Moses to rise among their people. The experience prepared Obama for the platform to serve his people. By divine appointment and at the appropriate time and season, he showed up on the scene to rescue the situation – at a time of economic meltdown, widespread home foreclosures, high unemployment, and widespread bank failures! You too can go for what God is calling you to.

Events Beyond Control

Moses was born in an era of trouble and unprecedented danger to his life. The enemy wanted him dead before he could see the light of day, but God wanted him alive. He had a great destiny on his life. In Exodus 2:2 the Bible says about Moses' mother that "when she saw that he was a fine child, she hid him for three months." This suggests that Moses' mother was inclined to keep him just because he was a fine child. Since babies are typically beautiful and adorable, what Moses' mother saw was beyond physical appearance of beauty. There was something special beyond the ordinary that signaled to her that this child must be preserved at all cost. There was something about the glory of God upon this child.

After three months of hiding her baby, she took him to the bank of the Nile River and placed him in a basket coated with tar and pitch to facilitate floatation. Her ingenuity is simply incredible since it was not common practice then to manufacture baby prams with such safety features. Her brilliant idea had to come from the divine!

While on the Nile, the more likely outcome would have been tragedy rather than rescue. Moses could have sunk, starved to death, or perhaps been discovered by an uncompassionate Egyptian. By divine appointment, the basket was guided toward Pharaoh's daughter, who happened to come out at the right time and with a compassionate state of mind. She listened to Miriam and accepted her suggestion to have a Hebrew woman take care of the baby at the Hebrew woman's house where the baby was still susceptible to great danger. Pharaoh's daughter's compassion toward Moses and her decision to adopt him and name him Moses (Exodus 2:10) were altogether orchestrated by divine providence and outside of Moses' parents' control.

Can you also imagine the significance of his name, Moses, meaning *drawn from the water*? Some of the great miracles done by God through Moses involved water. They include crossing of the Red Sea, getting water out of the rock, and healing the bitter water of Marah. Anything outside our control as we stay on the pathways to destiny is within God's control. It is important to note that God leaves some things within our control and to our discretion.

Some people wish they were born to more affluent parents or in certain geographical areas, or better still with specific opportunities that are available to others perceived better than them. It is futile to waste time and energy on circumstances outside our control. Instead, we need to think about the unique purposes for which we were created and our place within the special circumstances that surround us so as to seize the opportunities the times and seasons present. Accept those situations and circumstances that are outside your control, not as negative factors, but as part of God's design.

Marks on the Wall

By human appraisal, there were a series of events, circumstances, and encounters which when analyzed portrayed Moses as the ideal candidate for God's use in liberating the Hebrews. First among others was the fact that he was Hebrew. Secondly, as a Hebrew boy he gained favor and access very early in life to the palace of Pharaoh, where he was treated as a prince and with the niceties that went with royalty. He had access to the best formal education and leadership training at the time. In spite of the privileges and higher social status, Moses still identified with the Hebrews (Exodus 2:11, Hebrews 11:23-29) and their plight, though his upbringing and training would have made him pass for an Egyptian (Exodus 2:19). He was compassionate toward his people and had the inherent tendency to stand up in their defense, which further signaled that he was to play a crucial role in their liberation. Your passions, inclinations, and desires are powerful pointers to your destiny.

The marks on the wall became glaring when in Exodus 2:13-14 Moses was found resolving a dispute between two Hebrews. The insightful question they asked him was: "who made you prince and judge over us?" Moses' reaction seemed typical of the average person's selective hearing under similar circumstances. He did not hear the "prince and judge" that his fellow Hebrew men hinted at. Instead, he heard and responded to the question that followed: "...Are you thinking of killing me as you killed the Egyptian?" (Exodus 2:14). Yet we see later that God indeed chose Moses to be ruler and judge over Israel (Acts 7:35). Unknown to Moses, he was being prepared for a journey that lay ahead.

There was later a similar event when Moses encountered Jethro's daughters whom he helped against terrorizing shepherds (Exodus 2:16-17). He was repeatedly confronted with situations in which he felt inclined to help the weak. It was in him to step up into what God had planned for him to be – a deliverer!

The signs around you and the passion within, if you carefully discern them, could very well be marks on the wall, signaling you to what you may have been called to do. And even with occasional oppositions and encounters, if you would be careful enough and respond appropriately, you might very well find yourself moving closer to fulfilling your destiny.

In the case of Moses, the marks on the wall were more glaring considering the fact that he was not the only Hebrew child whose mother tried to keep him away from Pharaoh's slaughter, and he also was not the only male in his family. There was Aaron his elder brother, the elders, and possibly other strong men of stature who could have been raised up to confront Pharaoh and lead Israel out of Egypt. God did not choose any of those. He instead prepared Moses and inspired him specifically for the purpose of delivering Israel from Egyptian bondage.

Destiny beckons us and pulls us in the direction of our calling. It calls us out of the multitude to do what others might not be interested in. It makes us bold to take actions and do things that are unpremeditated, which we yet find ourselves inclined to do without much concern for the cost. There is always the temptation to follow the crowd or go down the path of least resistance. To follow the crowd is to choose to have your destiny in your control, which makes failure imminent. Choosing the difficult but necessary paths requires courage, and you will be amazed to find unexpected help attending your way.

Common questions to ponder in difficult times ought to be: How can I help others? How can I contribute to finding solutions to the momentary issue(s)? Benefits and gains tend to follow when the right path is chosen, and others are positively impacted. In the process of fulfilling your destiny, you may become wealthy and famous; however, those are usually not your driving force. The driving force for those on their pathways to fulfilling destiny is making lasting impact and bringing about much needed change in the lives of humankind among whom God places them. This is true of everyone who has left lasting footprints on the sands of time. It wouldn't be different for you.

Life Happens

It is imperative that we realize that life happens. Events occur, some within and others outside of our control. It is however equally important that we be assured that irrespective of what those events or issues might be, they quite possibly could be our steppingstones, helping to take us further and higher in the fulfillment of our destiny. Having proper perspective of life events and the ability to discern appropriate responses are key success factors over the challenges of such situations. We all need courage to step into the destiny God has for us. Additionally, we need to recognize our strengths and be mindful of how our desires and interests interconnect with our passion – without making money the primary motive – and cautiously proceed to do what we are called to do. Like the celebrated sons of Issachar (1 Chronicles 12:32), we need to covet wisdom and the ability to understand the times and seasons we are in. Personal discernment and/or counsel from those with the gift of discernment will always help.

Helpers

The sons of Issachar (1 Chronicles 12:32) had understanding of the times to know what Israel ought to do. At different occasions throughout the Bible, the prophets helped people know what to do in their journey to destiny. Spouses have also been known to play crucial roles in helping their partners fulfill their destiny. Examples include Zipporah (Moses' wife), Sarah (Abraham's wife), Joseph (Mary's husband), and many others who helped their spouses, sometimes behind the scenes. With self-centeredness always vaunting itself within families and communities, the wise man and woman will do well to listen to his/her spouse. The sons of Issachar, the prophets, the spouses, and many others were divine helpers raised at different times and seasons to help God's people.

From the onset of creation, God created Eve to be a suitable helper for Adam. He created our spouses to fulfill powerful roles toward the realization of our destinies. For example, God told Abraham to listen to his wife Sarah in Genesis 21:12. There have been instances in which the wife received divine revelation or visitation from God before her husband, including the wife of Manoah (Judges 13:3-6), Mary and her cousin Elizabeth (Luke 1), and numerous others. In the case of Rachel, wife of Isaac, she was the only one with information about the destiny of their children (Esau and Jacob).

Undoubtedly our spouses are instrumental in the fulfilling of our destiny, if after comparing and contrasting their counsels we have found them to align with the counsel and purpose of God for our lives. It is possible for a spouse's counsel to contradict the counsel of God. For example, Sarah counseled Abraham to take her maidservant, Hagar, (Genesis 16:1-4) for wife. You know the rest of the story and how that singular act has created eternal issues. Again, Adam should not have listened to Eve in the Garden of Eden. Through heeding her counsel, Adam fell (Genesis 3:1-24).

Parents and Parent Figures

Moses derived crucial understanding of leadership principles from his stepfather Jethro (Exodus 18). Ruth gained understanding of how to extend ancestry from Naomi, her mother-in-law (Ruth 3:1-18). Cousin Mordecai helped position Esther for ascension to the throne as queen and to gain understanding that led to the preservation of the Jews (Esther 2:20). Samuel learned how to hear from God through the understanding gained from Eli, his mentor and father figure (1 Samuel 3:7-9). Solomon gained wisdom and understanding to build and sustain his destiny from David (his father) and Bathsheba (his mother) as can be seen in Proverbs 1:8 and 4. The latter part of Solomon's life could not be said to be as successful. Solomon heeded the counsel of his parents pertaining to women when he started out but later acted contrary to their counsel. Samson was yet another one who paid dearly for not heeding the counsel of his parents (Judges 16).

Others

There are people with beneficial wisdom, knowledge, and/or understanding that do not occupy significant positions as parent, mentor, spouse, leader, financial advisor, etc., but are yet important on our journey to destiny. They have proven many times to be game-changers in circumstances that seemed challenging in the efforts at optimizing our potentials. David gained very helpful insight from Abigail when he was on the verge of bloodshed following the provocation by Nabal (1 Samuel 25:24). Another time an Egyptian helped David find his enemies in 1 Samuel 30:11-15. Naaman's servant provided him with invaluable insight that led to healing from leprosy (2 Kings 5:2-15).

The importance of having the right people around you cannot be overemphasized. It is of tremendous benefit to have the right people around us to answer questions such as: What is happening around me? In what direction is the tide turning? How do I fit in? What are the unique or rare qualities I possess or need to leverage at this time and season? What are my weaknesses or blind spots?

Prepare in Advance, Learn on the Job

Very few success stories involve someone being thrust into a position of destiny without prior experience–and none rely solely on the expertise of others. Most have had significant levels of preparation, sometimes unknown to them, for the position they later occupied. They would undoubtedly need to add to the experiences what they learn on the job as they go along.

In the light of destiny and purpose, everyone ought to be asking himself questions such as: What might the future hold? What skills and capabilities do I need to develop in order to be prepared? Unknown to Moses, his upbringing in the palace as well as the wilderness experience prepared him in no small way for the task ahead of him. The leadership principles he learned from Jethro, his father-in-law (Exodus 18:17-26), were complimentary on-the-job training that helped advance the realization of his destiny. Again, though Moses may not have known with certainty all that he needed for the task ahead, his severe tests at different seasons were indicative of and preparation for what to expect. When faced with difficult times in the wilderness, Moses was not caught by surprise. He had prior experience and preparation. As the saying goes, "He had been there and done that."

On the job, he learned how not to burn his candle at both ends. Before Jethro's counsel, he wasted his time and energy and was bogged down with little details instead of addressing the pressing national needs and setting the bigger picture. By implementing Jethro's counsel, Moses saved himself frustrations and aggravations and was able to move the nation forward toward their Promised Land as he delegated to trusted rulers and judges among his people.

The advance preparation, and his ability to present a teachable spirit as he learned on the job, made it easier for Moses to leave the affairs of state and go up to Mount Sinai to spend time with God and receive the Ten Commandments and establish the Old Testament laws (Exodus 19:3, 20). It enabled him to be positioned for further elevation (Exodus 19:9). He could then focus more attention on setting up the priesthood, writing the Pentateuch, and preparing the people for entry into the Promised Land.

Everyone's learning needs are different. So also are individual aptitude and temperaments under different learning conditions. Preparation for future success involves ongoing learning. Continuous learning helps with current responsibilities and can help prepare for future challenges and opportunities. Challenges and opportunities evolve, and so also must learning how to meet them. These dynamics involve formal and informal education, experience, networking, and self-awareness leading to the formation of new habits and much more.

Moses' Shortcoming

God intended for Moses to enter the Promised Land from the beginning of the exodus. However, God also has standards no one should take for granted – including Moses. When Moses in his anger killed the Egyptian soldier (Exodus 2:11-12), God was not pleased. When that same anger led to the smashing of the first set of tablets (Exodus 32:19, 22) God was not pleased either. That was a temperament God endured but which Moses needed to deal with.

Furthermore, Moses could have been better at pointing Israel to God rather than to himself. They saw him as their deliverer and not Yahweh, the Almighty God (Exodus 32:23). There was also the obvious lapse in delegation of authority as even Aaron his elder brother was inadequately prepared for the challenges in his forty-day absence (Exodus 32:22-25).

Unbridled temperaments (and habits) not dealt with soon enough will bring the best of leaders down. Dr. Howard Dean, for example, could not make the presidential nomination because of his inability to moderate his temper during political rallies. The same goes for Herman Cain, John Edwards, Mark Spitzer, and others, whose unbridled temperaments and idiosyncrasies brought them down from positions of glory. And shortcomings do not have boundaries nor are they limited to political office holders. Spiritual leaders and marketplace leaders have prematurely ended, or at best derailed their destinies, as a result of excesses, including sexual immorality and other uncorrected weaknesses. They failed to deal with obvious shortcomings and allowed many to continue to rub their ego until they experienced freefall.

I cannot overemphasize the importance of having periodic self-assessments and the need to courageously confront the weakness that plagues you before it has its full hold on you with adverse consequences. You also must learn to delegate responsibilities and allow commensurate authority through constant and continuous on-the-job training of yourself and your subordinates. Think big and increase your capacity by elevating trusted subordinates.

Chapter questions:
1. What is the one thing you would do if you had the power and resources to change situations and circumstances around you? What is your dominant passion and heart's cry?

2. What issue(s) in my local or global community do I feel compelled to bring solution(s) to?

3. How can I help others? How can I contribute to finding solutions to the momentary issue(s)?

4. Where do I fit in the current issue happening around me?

5. What are the unique qualities I possess that needs to be leveraged at this time and season of my life?

6. What are my weaknesses or blind spots? What must I do to address those weaknesses and blind spots? You may need to get trusted aides to help mitigate your weaknesses and blind spots.

Chapter Nine:

The Journey to Destiny

"Thus says the LORD: 'Stand in the ways and see, and ask for the old paths, where the good way is, and walk in it; then you will find rest for your souls'..."
– Jeremiah 6:16 (KJV)

"Destiny is not a matter of chance but a matter of choice. It is not a thing to be waited for; it is a thing to be achieved."
– William Jennings Bryan

Destiny is not a straight path or an event but a lifelong journey with multiple pathways and events. As with any journey, the desired destination, the paths traveled, the signs along the way, decisions made along the way, the travel companions, counsels received when directions are sought, and determination to get to your destination all have critical roles to play in the outcome of your journey. The uncertainties surrounding your journey are so great, as are the variety of possible outcomes, that you cannot leave your destiny to chance. You need to know where you are going and get the resources and guidance necessary to help you reach the finish line. When you embark on a journey toward destiny, you never know what uncertainties you will encounter, or what curveballs life will throw your way. You are usually not forewarned of the threats and opportunities life will present.

In light of the uncertainties of life, which are beyond your control, you need divine guidance and interventions along the way. God Almighty has the greatest desire to see us fulfill our destiny, and He is always willing and well able to help us along the pathways to our destiny.

Destiny's Progressive Phases

David was chosen among his brothers and anointed (1 Samuel 16:13) but did not foresee this significant display of divine favor coming his way. There is no indication from careful study of the biblical narrative that David was being anointed as king. He could have been anointed to function as prophet, priest, or any other prominent role among his people. This assertion is underscored by the fact that Jesse subsequently sent David on an errand to his brothers in the camp where they were fighting the Philistines (see 1 Samuel 17:17-19). Had Jesse known of God's plan for David's future, he probably would not have exposed him to what would have been seen as danger, but was opportunity in reality.

David did not understand the significance of his anointing by Samuel. How does a person go from being a mere shepherd boy caring for his father's sheep in the field to being put on a path to the throne as king of one of the most powerful kingdoms on earth? There is clearly a great distinction between shepherd (caring for sheep) and king ruling over a kingdom filled with people, of which there are many great and mighty personalities. In spite of the odds, David would cross the seemingly insurmountable schism as a mere shepherd boy to arrive at God's chosen destiny for him. But this journey would be unveiled over a lengthy process of time, in phases.

We advance in our journey to our God-given destinies in phases. Life events are not always as they appear on the surface. In 1 Samuel 16:13, we see that upon being anointed, the Spirit of God came mightily upon David and set him on the true path of his destiny. Meanwhile, "the Spirit of the Lord departed from Saul, and a distressing spirit from the Lord troubled him" (1 Samuel 16:14), and the solution to Saul's problem was David. This event ushered David to the next phase of his life, with firsthand exposure to the nitty-gritty of life in the king's palace as an armor bearer to the king with tremendous favor (1 Samuel 17:21-22). In 1 Samuel 17, with the Goliath challenge came the opportunity to step up to the next phase of David's destiny.

With God in our lives, we can expect events to be divinely orchestrated with the purpose of moving us further along toward fulfilling our destiny. In those events, we find ourselves suited to provide solutions to problems while given the opportunity to advance to the next phase of our destiny.

David went from being insignificant to inheriting glory and greatness, not through his own efforts and abilities but by divine guidance and help. In David's quest to fulfill his destiny, he met with all sorts of unique challenges, oppositions, and distasteful events along the way. Yet, because he knew God and was a man after God's heart, every step he took brought him closer to destiny, even when he did not know what it was all about – at the time. At various points in his journey to significance, David could have given up, especially when he had to run for his life away from Saul and wander in the wilderness. He could have thought his situation hopeless and the perceived destiny unattainable. Doubt could have crept in as he wondered if the prophet made a mistake in anointing him after all. Perhaps fear, a major destiny killer, would have seized the opportunity to invade David's mind and to cripple his hope of ever accomplishing God's plan for his life. Experiences similar to this are not unique to David. Perhaps you can relate to David's experiences. It is inevitable that at various phases of our journey through life, as we make efforts at fulfilling our destinies, we will face disturbing issues that may threaten the realization of our destinies.

After prevailing against Goliath, for instance, David had to go through the wilderness experience where he learned valuable lessons. That was where he developed diplomatic relations with the Philistines and built a great army of battle-tested loyalists. As David was completing one phase of his journey, he progressed to the next. The phases are different for different people. You may need to go back to school and learn certain skills. You may need to be mentored in a particular discipline or gain experience and acquire certain skills that will help you further in the pathways to your destiny.

David's multifaceted experience in the journey to destiny is typical of the average person. Everyone faces varying degrees of obstacles and threats to the realization of our destinies. Fortunately, what is impossible for men to accomplish is always possible for God. It is only logical and wise then to get to know and walk with this God who is able to bring those obstacles and threats under subjection. While teaching His disciples about the kingdom of heaven, Jesus recognized the difficulty of getting into God's kingdom (a desirable eternal destination) by a person's natural efforts but concluded that "with men this is impossible, but with God all things are possible" (Matthew 19:26). God told Paul: "My grace is sufficient for you, for my strength is made perfect in your weakness" (2 Corinthians 12:9). It is imperative to lean on God's grace and strength in our weaknesses and vulnerabilities as we go through the process of fulfilling our destiny.

It could be harrowing to journey through life leaning on your understanding and knowledge. Imagine seeing someone who got lost on his way to a particular destination and refused to seek help or ask for direction. Such a person may either never get to their destination or might get there very late. Or perhaps imagine this lost person asking the wrong person for direction, who instead of admitting not knowing the way, points him in the wrong direction. It is certain that our lost friend will either not get to his destination or arrive too late and with a lot of avoidable distress.

Rather than trust in yourself or in others that do not quite know the way, it makes a lot of sense to "Trust in the LORD with all your heart, and lean not on your own understanding; in all your ways acknowledge Him, and He [the Lord] shall direct your paths" (Proverbs 3:5-6).

A fundamental lesson that can be learned from David and several great characters in the Bible and throughout history is that destinies originate from God, and "it is God who works in you both to will and to do of His good pleasure" (Philippians 2:13). Your destiny is typically bigger than your dream or desired future and thus can't be achieved solely by your own efforts and available resources. God's destiny, plans, and purposes for your life are always much greater than you and might seem, in the natural, unattainable. However, you must relax as the destiny giver is well able to bring it together and make it a reality – if you will *trust* and *lean on* Him.

David surrendered completely to God. He trusted in God, not leaning on his own limited understanding (Psalm 23). In turn, God helped David every step of the way through pleasant and distasteful experiences till He brought him to the place of fulfillment. You need God to help you get to your destiny. He will – if you will learn to trust Him, acknowledge Him, and lean on Him.

When David encountered Goliath, God helped him. God was with him when he was under severe attack and in great danger in the house of Saul, his father-in law, whom he defeated Goliath for and for whom he got rid of the distressing spirit that was troubling him. God was there when David was in the wilderness, surrounded by men considered to be hopeless and downtrodden. God was still in control when David was looked down upon and disregarded by many, including Nabal, who had the effrontery to say "who is David? Who is the son of Jesse? There are many servants nowadays who break away each one from his master" (1 Samuel 25:10). This was said of someone who was anointed and had proved to be a champion in Israel (for killing Goliath).

Circumstances and words like those breed discouragement and could cripple the strongest of wills. David, like most people, had moments of doubt and discouragement—moments when becoming king seemed unattainable. These were difficult phases in his journey toward realizing his destiny, but God was with him all the way. His journey to destiny was a process and not a singular event. After being crowned king, events continued to unravel, each one marking important milestones toward fulfilling his destiny. One step after the other, David trusted God to help him accomplish all that he could not do for himself.

History is replete – both in the Bible and in today's contemporary world – with stories of people that were despised or told they could never attain to anything significant in life. People that by the circumstances of life were consigned to failure but went on nonetheless to accomplish great things. They include people like Moses (Exodus 2), Isaiah (Isaiah 6:5-8), Jesus Christ (John 1, see v. 46), Walt Disney (1901-1966), President Abraham Lincoln (1809-1865), and several others.

Like David, you need God. As you lean on God, you will be amazed to see the picture of your destiny gradually but surely unfold before your very eyes. Keep your eyes on God. Be vigilant to attend to the instructions He gives you along the way. Follow the paths He directs you to and the warnings and alerts He brings to your attention. If you do, He will help you fulfill His plan and purpose concerning you.

Destiny and the Ungodly

People often ask why it is that people who do not know God appear to prosper. There are a number of reasons.

First it is helpful to realize that fulfilling one's destiny is not about attaining to position and acquiring wealth but living out God's premeditated plan, which involves having positive impact on the lives of others. Destiny should not be mistaken for accumulation of material things, which are without lasting value. Wealth and positions do not guarantee fulfillment and cannot be the evidence that someone is fulfilling his destiny. Mahatma Gandhi, Martin Luther, Martin Luther King Jr., Mother Teresa, and so forth may not have accumulated much wealth, relatively speaking, but discovered the paths to their destinies and left lasting impacts that outlive them. Among those that are fulfilling their destiny today are some who are Christians and trust in God. There are others who are not. But one common factor is the application of Christian principles which enables them to leave a positive impact on the sands of life. The distinction between Christians and non-Christians that fulfill their destiny here on earth is their eternal destination – life after death.

Everyone has a God-ordained destiny irrespective of their faith or lack thereof. Non-Christians who discover their calling in life can fulfill their destiny and find fulfillment while doing it. This is totally distinct from the matter of salvation in Christ. In Ezra, for example, the Bible records how God used a heathen king to accomplish His plans: "Now in the first year of Cyrus king of Persia, that the word of the LORD by the mouth of Jeremiah might be fulfilled, the LORD stirred up the spirit of Cyrus king of Persia, so that he made a proclamation throughout all his kingdom, and also put it in writing, saying, Thus says Cyrus king of Persia: All the kingdoms of the Earth the LORD God of heaven has given me. And He has commanded me to build Him a house at Jerusalem which is in Judah. Who is among you of all His people? May his God be with him, and let him go up to Jerusalem which is in Judah, and build the house of the LORD God of Israel (He is God), which is in Jerusalem" (Ezra 1:1-3).

True fulfillment on earth comes only when we are able to satisfy the instinctive desire, burden, or urge (calling) that we feel. Your means of income, and whatever the vocation is in itself, is not the end. Wealth, career accomplishments, and so on are avenues to help you fulfill the deep yearnings or passion that God has placed in your heart. Pursuing material things without attending to your God-given yearning can be compared to being offered soda or juice when you are in reality thirsty for pure water. It will not quench your thirst or satisfy you – no matter how sweet. In just the same way, money and position are "sweet," but without attending to your God-given plans, you cannot attain your destiny.

Wealth and positions can be baits that have often distracted many people from pursuing God's plans for their lives. Jesus said to His followers, "Take heed and beware of covetousness, for one's life does not consist in the abundance of the things he possesses" (Luke 12:15). Wealth and position for true Christians are byproducts to pursuing and fulfilling destiny. Jesus admonishes believers in Matthew 6:33 to "seek first the kingdom of God and His righteousness, and all these things shall be added to you." So do not be envious of unbelievers who appear to be prospering by human standards (see Psalm 37:7, Proverbs 23:17-18). Instead, seek for the materialization of God's will in your life.

Secondly, God has put unbiased universal principles in effect, such as the principle of sowing and reaping that applies to everyone (Christians and non-Christians). Jesus makes it clear in Matthew 5:2, "… for He makes His sun rise on the evil and on the good, and sends rain on the just and on the unjust." God in His infinite goodness and mercy distributes certain benefits to all people. The laws and principles of God work for all. For example, the law of reproduction gives the ability for a mature healthy couple (married or unmarried man and woman) to have children. God's principles and laws are not prejudiced. While He allows the principles to work, He punishes underlying sins such as adultery and fornication that may be associated with the reproduction of offspring by illegitimate couples, if they do not repent. Universal laws and divine principles are not biased and cannot be overturned.

Thirdly, those who are Christians and grounded in righteousness can expect that God will allow the ungodly to labor, toil, and store up goods for the benefit of the righteous. Even if the righteous men or women never get to truly experience material blessings in their lifetime, they can expect blessings which are byproducts of their kingdom work to accrue to their posterity. "A good [righteous] man leaves an inheritance [spiritual or physical; tangible or intangible] to his children's children, but the wealth of the sinner is stored up for the righteous" (Proverbs 13:22).

God allowed the Canaanites to remain in the land He promised to the offspring of Abraham (Genesis 12), and even though Jacob (Abraham's grandson) migrated from the land to Egypt, his posterity repossessed the land and benefitted from the labor of the Canaanites. While the Canaanites inhabited the land, they had a false perception of ownership because it was only a matter of time before the true owners would emerge to take possession. The same concept holds true for the unrighteous in possession of wealth. Those who are rich outside of God are storing up riches for the righteous and their posterity (Proverbs 13:22).

As you identify your God-given passion and the paths He has laid out for you, start taking steps toward fulfilling them. You have within you certain endowments that distinguish you from others. The adage goes that "a journey of a thousand miles begins with a step." Every great inventor and reformer started off small but followed their passions. Some started in a certain direction and ended with outstanding results never anticipated. In the process of inventing something in particular, they stumbled upon discoveries that brought them greater fulfillment. Unknown to them, however, these were part of the larger fulfillment of destiny.

Examples include Thomas Edison, who invented the light bulb after several failures. Out of the light bulb failures, he went on to several other inventions. The Wright Brothers made the first flight. Benjamin Franklin discovered electricity and invented the Franklin stove. Alexander Bell invented the telephone. Leonardo Da Vinci, who is noted as one of the greatest minds ever, invented models that proved workable thirty-five hundred years later. These notable figures made several attempts before eventually succeeding – both in their time and sometimes after they were long gone. The result of their pursuit of passion succeeded them and has benefitted mankind on a large scale.

The same could be said of early church reformers who followed their passions against all odds and went on to make profound difference in the world. Their lives were often in great danger, yet they had the courage to pursue their God-given passions. These early reformers include the following personalities:

Pope Gregory VII (1015–1085) instituted a series of ground-breaking reforms known as the Gregorian Reforms that dealt with the moral integrity and independence of the clergy. The Gregorian Reforms furthered the collections of canon law that were being assembled, in order to buttress the papal position, during the same period. He also helped the church avoid slipping back into the seriously embarrassing abuses that had occurred in Rome during the Rule of the Harlots, between 900 and 1050. In a time of turmoil and uncertainty of the continuity of the Roman Catholic Church, Gregory helped with necessary reforms and thereby preserved the church.

John Wycliffe (1320–1384). Wycliffe opposed what he perceived as corruption within the church, including the sale of indulgences, pilgrimages, the excessive veneration of saints, and the low moral and intellectual standards of ordained priests. In his journey to destiny, Wycliffe courageously repudiated the doctrine of transubstantiation, asserted that the Bible was the sole standard of Christian doctrine, and argued that the authority of the pope was not grounded in Scripture. He set the stage that allowed some of his early followers to translate the Bible into English, while later followers, known as Lollards, held that the Bible was the sole authority and that Christians were called upon to interpret the Bible for themselves. The Lollards were also known to have argued against clerical celibacy, transubstantiation, mandatory oral confession, pilgrimages, and indulgences.

Martin Luther (1483–1546). In 1517, Martin Luther nailed his "Ninety-Five Theses" onto a Wittenberg Church door. His theses were Latin propositions opposing the manner in which indulgences (release from the temporal penalties for sin through the payment of money) were being sold in order to raise money for the building of Saint Peter's basilica in Rome. Like Wycliffe, Luther was opposed to a very powerful institution but determined to travel his God-ordained path, and he fulfilled his destiny.

John Calvin (1509–1564). Calvin was a French theologian and reformer who fled religious persecution in France and settled in Geneva in 1536. He instituted a form of church government in

Geneva which gave birth to the Presbyterian Church. Calvin insisted on reforms including: the congregational singing of the Psalms as part of church worship, the teaching of a catechism and confession of faith to children, and the enforcement of a strict moral discipline in the community by the pastors and members of the church. Geneva was essentially a theocracy because Calvin dared to follow his passion.

Henry VIII (1491–1547). Henry Tudor was the main instigator of the English Reformation. In 1533, Henry was excommunicated by the pope for marrying Anne Boleyn and having the Archbishop of Canterbury sanction the divorce from his first wife, Catherine. In 1534, Henry had Parliament pass an act appointing the king and his successors as supreme head of the Church of England, thus establishing an independent national Anglican Church. Though Henry was involved in ungodly deeds, he was somehow in tune with God's corporate destiny for the church in England. Consequently, I believe that God used him to liberate the church from the corruption of the church in Rome.

The aforementioned examples of some of the early reformers are by no means an attempt to promote or degrade any particular denomination. The lives of these reformers bear testimony of their focus and determination to fulfill what they considered their passions. They courageously pursued their passions and altered the status quo of their time. This should encourage you to pursue your passions. Start by taking baby steps today. Just like the great inventors and reformers, as you begin to take steps in the direction of fulfilling your destiny—as you pursue your interests and passions—you will find great doors opening to you with the help of God.

Information

When God called the Israelites out of Egypt, He told Moses that He would harden Pharaoh's heart. Moses did not know the significance and implication of this and went to Pharaoh not knowing how events would unfold with the powerful king whose heart God would harden. He was not privy to the number of plagues that God would put on the Egyptians, the lag between each plague, the reaction of various stakeholders along the way, or any other information of events that would transpire as he traveled God's path for his life.

The absence of detailed information disclosure by God, as we journey to our destiny, is often a blessing in disguise. It is in itself a function of God's grace. Inasmuch as knowledge has great benefits, it could also be detrimental. Though hard to imagine, we might be better off not having certain information. God reveals information to us based on the need to know. "The secret things belong to the LORD our God, but those things which are revealed belong to us and to our children forever, that we may do all the words of this law" (Deuteronomy 29:29). All Moses needed to know was God's assurance that He would bring the Israelites out of Egypt to a predestined place. The other events in between would unfold phase by phase and stage by stage – in accordance with God's plans and purposes.

The same applies to us. Once we get a glimpse of where God is taking us, we don't have to worry about the details. We should be ready to go through the multifaceted high and low phases without attempting to skip ahead (you don't know where to skip to anyway) and trust God to bring us to the destination He has already prepared for us.

Enjoy the ride with the assurance that: "all things work together for good to those who love God, to those who are the called according to His purpose" (Romans 8:28). If you heed God's voice and follow in the direction of His calling, you can be sure that every experience along the way will advance you and bring you closer to your destiny. When you encounter bumps along the road to destiny, remember God's Word that says "I know the thoughts that I think toward you, says the LORD, thoughts of peace and not of evil, to give you a future and a hope" (Jeremiah 29:11).

As with any journey, you may encounter heavy traffic along the way and find yourself in a holding pattern. Be patient. When you experience inclement weather on the way and find the horizon to be cloudy, know that it is time to proceed cautiously. You may have a flat, which indicates that it is time to take a break and make some fixes. When you have excellent visibility and permission to speed up, then step on the pedal and go for it. Whatever the conditions you encounter along the way, "count it all joy" as James admonished (James 1:2). The Israelites finished well on the journey to their destiny because God spoke and they cooperated.

In Exodus 12:31-36 God instructed the Israelites to demand articles of gold and silver but did not make known the reasons. Oftentimes God does not fully tell us what He wants to do – for our own benefit. Wisdom demands that we follow Him nonetheless one step at a time. He could have asked the Israelites to get ready to plunder the Egyptians or to borrow from them with the knowledge that those valuables would not be returned. He simply told them to ask. Additional information beyond this could have resulted in confusion, betrayal, and avoidable complications. God saved the people from themselves as it would only take one Israelite to ruin things for the others. Knowing everything in advance could create its own burden, as we could carelessly disclose it to our enemies unawares or maybe even create a state of anxiety for ourselves and others.

It is my opinion that if Jesus had told the disciples everything about their future experiences, and the eternal implications of His death on the cross in advance of His death, it would have been difficult for Judas to betray Jesus as Satan himself would have done everything he could to protect Jesus rather than have Judas betray Jesus – as it had been written. The reason for this point is that Jesus' death on the cross made a way for the propitiation of sin and redemption of mankind. That was bad news for Satan, who did not see this coming.

A crucial lesson from the Exodus narrative is that God chose the timing at which the last plague would be unleashed — at *nighttime*. This was a time when the Egyptians would be most vulnerable, caught off guard, unsuspecting, and unable to see the Israelites departing with their valuables. God chooses the timing of crucial events in our lives and works out the strategies for our breakthroughs. It is natural to wonder about when certain things will work out for us, when we can expect our break, and to ponder other uncertainties surrounding our lives. What you should be concerned about mainly is whether or not God is in control of your life. If He is, and you continue to let Him be, rest assured that He will choose the perfect timing to work things out for your good and will never be late a minute! He is always on time, and nothing catches Him by surprise. He is the Good Shepherd that brings His sheep to the prepared place of rest and fulfillment. As you follow Him, be content with the amount of information God chooses to reveal to you. Have faith in God.

Trust His expediency.

At the time of God's choosing, Pharaoh, who hitherto had a hardened heart, suddenly had a change of heart and a sense of urgency to let Israel go (Exodus 13:12). In the same way, God's timing will be perfect with you. What's more, Israel did not have to do anything special. They did not have to fire a single gunshot or show some extraordinary strength. They simply did what God instructed them to do through Moses. God orchestrated the rest – just as Zechariah was to later prophesy: "This is the word of the LORD to Zerubbabel: 'Not by might nor by power, but by My Spirit,' says the LORD of hosts" (Zechariah 4:6). As you stay on the path that God has for you, and do what He expects of you, time will prove God's faithfulness to you.

Furthermore, we are told in Exodus 14:5 that Pharaoh was informed that the people (Israel) had fled, which was appropriate since Moses only told Pharaoh they were going into the wilderness to worship God. He did not disclose that they were leaving permanently. Pharaoh had no clue of what God intended to do, nor did he understand the magnitude of God's plan for Israel. When Pharaoh got a hint of what God was doing with Israel, he changed his mind and was once again in opposition to God's plan, Israel's destiny. Could you imagine hell breaking loose in order to stop the destiny of a people who hitherto had followed the leading of a faithful God? At that very time, God took responsibility for ensuring the success of Israel's departure, and He will always do the same for those who follow Him. When you are faced with opposition and not sure how events would turn, trust God and hold your peace. Jesus said to the disciples, "Follow Me, and I will make you become fishers of men" (Mark 1:17).

God takes responsibility for ensuring the best possible outcome for those who choose to follow Him completely. He never promises a smooth and seamless journey in life. However, He guarantees to be there for you to ensure that you fulfill your destiny and finish well. Moses said to the Israelites as they continued onward to their destiny: "And the LORD, He is the One who goes before you. He will be with you; He will not leave you nor forsake you; do not fear nor be dismayed" (Deuteronomy 31:8). With the knowledge that challenges will always be present and that you do not have to know the details, be prepared to forge ahead and never retreat. Determine in your mind to go all the way. Keep your eyes on the finish line (the place of great joy and fulfillment) as Paul counseled in Philippians 3:13 and Hebrews 2:1.

Should you ever get to the edge of the Red Sea and the crossroads of life, trust completely in God and listen for instructions. Do not turn back or "chicken out" as many tend to do. Be tenacious like Queen Esther, who would rather die trying to fulfill her destiny than betray her people (see Esther 4:16). Be courageous and have a strong faith attitude. Follow God and desire always to please Him.

On a last note in this chapter, I would like to encourage you just as Jesus did in response to a reluctant prospective disciple who wanted to follow Him but desired first to attend to other matters. "...Jesus said to him, 'No one, having put his hand to the plow, and looking back, is fit for the kingdom of God'" (Luke 9:62). Why would God take Israel through the Red Sea, you might want to ask? Being omniscient, He knew they would want to turn back if confronted by hard challenges. So He took them through the Red Sea, realizing that once they crossed the sea there would be no turning back.

The less inclined you are to turn away from confronting your destiny because of life's challenges, the less likely the chances of being presented with Red Seas to cross. When faced with difficulty along the way and tempted to retreat to status quo, remember what Jesus said in Luke 9:62 – and don't look back. Stay focused on your path to fulfilling your destiny and be alert for divine guidance and revelation. We will deal with the topic of divine guidance and revelation later on in this book.

Exercise on your journey to destiny:
1. What are your passions, urges, or innate desires? If money was not an option, what are some things you would be doing?

2. What has God asked, or is asking, you to do that you have not started because you are waiting for more instructions and detail? What baby steps can you begin to take?

3. How would you describe your walk with God? On a scale of 1-10, candidly rate your relationship under God's control - with 10 being excellent and 1 being the least. How would you rate God's control over your life? What disciplines (such as Bible study, praying, and fellowship) do you need to commit to starting today in order to have a "10" point rating?

4. What challenges are you currently facing in your life's journey? Write them down, and prayerfully hand them over to God. Be assured that He knows precisely what to do.

Chapter Ten:

Clues from The Past

"Remember the days of old, consider the years of many generations. Ask your father, and he will show you; your elders, and they will tell you"
– Deuteronomy 32:7

"I felt as if I were walking with destiny, and that all my past life had been but a preparation for this hour and this trial."
– Winston Churchill

The past, the present, and the future are all interrelated. Irrespective of where you are today, there is nothing you can do to change or alter your past successes, failures, achievements, and disappointments. You cannot undo discussions, unsay words spoken, or alter things that were done. Careful attention to the events of the past provides support for today's successes and clues to future possibilities. Our past actions and inactions leave trails that point to the destination we are likely to wind up at. While we must never dwell in the past, live under the guilt of our errors and omissions, or on the euphoria of our successes, we can learn valuable lessons from the past that could guide our today and shape our future.

Past experiences are like landmarks and signposts that point to what has been, what we can learn from what has been, and how we can replicate successes and avoid failures. If for any reason you either get stuck or derailed on your pathway and become unsure where you are heading, it will be of tremendous benefit to look back at where you started, where you have been, what turns you took, where you had determined to go, and question yourself why you took those turns and what you should do to retrace your steps. However, you could be heading for a real disaster if you failed to heed all the warning signs that indicate you are on the wrong path and yet keep speeding toward the destination called "nowhere."

If you are not very familiar with the landscape and come across signs that suggest you are approaching "Canton" after a long drive from Chicago, you may get confused as to whether you are in Canton, Massachusetts, or Canton, Georgia. However, you will know where you are and where you are heading based on the reference points on your journey informed by where you have been. The peculiar routes you have traveled and landmarks you encountered along the way will give you the clues that you are on the proper course. In the journey to your destiny, past experiences hold crucial clues to where you are and where you are heading. They also help you determine whether to continue or make adjustments.

The attempt on Moses' life at birth by Pharaoh and the supernatural deliverance by God, forming his much needed past experiences of life, reassured Moses of God's intention, desire, and ability to supernaturally protect him from Pharaoh, or any king for that matter, should a similar experience occur in the future.

Contrary to common disclaimers in the investment management industry that "past performance is not indicative of future results," in the life of Moses and in a greater spiritual sense past performances are strong indicators of future results. Our individual and family histories and past experiences hold important clues about our futures. Your parents and ancestors have certain predispositions that you should consider, as these have bearing on your destiny. Abraham, Isaac, and Jacob received promises from God with lasting implications for generations yet unborn. It is not impossible that Moses and/or the scribes of his time read from the scrolls kept away by their forebears concerning God's promise to Abraham four hundred years prior, regarding their exodus from the land of bondage.

Being told of his miraculous birth and adoption by Pharaoh's family; seeing the spread-out plagues on the land of Egypt; the deaths of the firstborn; the wonderful liberation from Egypt and almost unbelievable transfer of the Egyptians' wealth to the Hebrews; the parting of the Red Sea – these past experiences convinced Moses that the God who did all these miracles could and would do similar or greater things if need be. He certainly must have known that those experiences were not coincidental. He knew he was born and groomed for such a time as that. The same could be said of Esther, Nehemiah, Daniel, Nehemiah, Ezra, and others in the Bible.

Clues from past experiences work in concert with the two other essentials, time and season, to advance the fulfillment of our destiny. Clues from the past help us assess our present position and prepare us for future opportunities whose time and season form integral parts of our destiny. Past experiences are for our preparation, and their relevance to time and season translates into necessary action. Adequate preparation from our past experience in conjunction with seizing opportunities at the right time and season is a key factor to fulfilling destiny.

Waiting periods ("wildernesses") of our life's journey are formative times for reflection and preparation. Such times bring about necessary opportunities in our preparation. They also enable us to harness acquired skills and knowledge in order to steer us into the future. Success is struck at the intersection of preparation and opportunity.

To have embarked on this book project five years earlier would have been impossible because I needed to study more of the Bible, needed more control in my schedule, and needed to experience more of the ebbs and flows of life. I needed these experiences to inform me as the Lord had it as part of my purpose to write on the subject of destiny. I consider it the right time as the Lord stirred up a conversation by divine appointment and gave me the opportunity and passion to write on the subject matter. I was also encouraged to stay focused of this project when I got distracted because it is a subject matter that I got interested in quite early in life. Linking clues from the past with strong conviction and insight to write on destiny encouraged me to stay on course.

Rest assured that when the timing is right to step forward into your destiny, you will know it because there will be an alignment of your passions, interests, opportunities, and inner conviction.

Additionally, as you look back to your past experiences for clues, be mindful of unfulfilled prophecies and uncompleted projects in the lives of your parents and/or grandparents in the areas that you sense the call of God upon your life. Moses summoned the people in Deuteronomy 32:7: "ask your father and your elders, they will tell you." Find out if there were things spoken over your life by credible individuals with appropriate authority during pregnancy or as a child. Ascertain the unique attributes you exhibited while growing up. Remember the things that you enjoyed doing and excelled in. These will help in no small way to motivate you toward fulfilling your destiny.

A clue from my past was an inordinate interest to learn about destiny at the age of twelve. I read literature of various kinds, including religious and philosophical writings, to find out if I was on the right path to fulfilling my destiny. For me back then, to fulfill one's destiny was to have possessions. I erroneously thought that having possessions translated into living a fulfilled life. Though my motive was off, the underlying question on how to fulfill destiny was imperative and formed a great part of this undertaking to find out the pathways to destiny so I could share with others in a similar predicament, using the authoritative Word of God as a framework.

Other clues from my past pertained to my interest in reading and pursuit of knowledge, which earned me the nickname "Mr. Know It All" among my friends. I tended to take a leadership role with friends and in the classroom. I was interested in knowing about God and often pondered the mysteries of creation and life. I enjoyed debating as a kid, in spite of the fact that I was not much of a communicator. And even then I noticed that people wanted to listen to me when I spoke. My opinions and inputs were often sought after. In a culture that places much value on age, I found it interesting that my older siblings and relatives often sought my input on a number of important matters prior to making decisions. Those were clues that I never gave much thought to but should have. Looking at the totality of my past and the trajectory of my future now, I can say with some degree of certainty that I have the seeds of leadership and have always had the inquisitive mind to seek answers to questions most people consider complex and to offer solutions.

My past experience also showed me that everlasting solutions must have their basis on the true and infallible Word of God. Now

I know that I am on track to doing what I was primarily created to do, with the Word of God as foundation.

Trust me when I say there are helpful clues from your past that will point you in the right path when you come to major crossroads in life. Many successful inventors were once kids who had an unusual interest in figuring out how things were created. They had creativity traits and very possibly a penchant to disassemble and reassemble their childhood toys. Some of those kids were misinterpreted to be destructive, as others did not know their inquisitive minds were waiting to be satisfied and redirected to more constructive exploits.

Parents need to carefully watch their young ones for signs that tend toward discernible traits of productivity instead of coercing them into pursuing careers and dreams that they (parents) deemed prestigious or with potential financial advantage. Children so coerced develop into adults who turn out to be unhappy in life, especially so if the parents' wishes do not align with the children's destiny.

The total picture of what a child might be is often not so clear, but from one point to another there will always be clues that point to his/her destiny. Parents need to be patient in observing those clues, starting with the child's passion and other inherent interests. It should not be difficult for parents to discover from these clues what lies ahead for their children.

Parents must understand that every child is unique and special. An important fiduciary responsibility of parents, as custodians of the tender and precious lives in their care, is to identify their unique inherent attributes and to help develop them rather than prod them on to their own preferred path. Parents should have a healthy respect for their children's interests and inclinations, while exposing them to different possibilities. Those interests that are supposedly for short-term use will fade, giving way to those that will stay with the children into adulthood. It is also imperative that parents commit their children to God in prayer and instruct them in the ways of God.

Jacob's Destiny Clues

Jacob was born a supplanter, as many referred to him (Genesis 27:36). Often overlooked are those clues present during Rebekah's pregnancy with Jacob and his bother Esau. In Genesis 25:22, we observe that while Rebekah was pregnant with twins, "the children struggled together within her." This was one of many crucial clues that would play out in the lives of the twins later in life. The clue was pointing to an exception in the ancient Jewish law of primogeniture that provided that in normal circumstances the younger would be subservient to the older. The abnormality in Rebekah's pregnancy was the first clue to the exception in the law governing birthright. At that point, in the mother's womb, it was easy for the clues of life to be ignored, but Rebekah was wise enough to inquire of the Lord in order to understand what that clue meant.

In Genesis 25:23 we read, "And the Lord said to her: Two nations are in your womb, two peoples shall be separated from your body; one people shall be stronger than the other, and the older shall serve the younger." Rebekah received understanding of the clue at pregnancy and gained insight into the destinies of her unborn boys. As is typical of God, He left out details about the path to which Jacob would fulfill his destiny. And as is typical with parents, Rebekah later mapped out a plan to help her beloved Jacob fulfill his destiny by conspiring to trick Isaac into blessing Jacob instead of Esau (Genesis 27:5-30). That was not necessary since the birthright already belonged to Jacob, and Esau had deliberately already sold his birthright to Jacob anyway (Genesis 25:29-33). When Esau sold his birthright, he also relinquished all the privileges and blessings of the first son to Jacob.

It is my belief that destiny will find the right context and opportunity – whether or not prodded by human hands. Esau willingly giving up his birthright due to a temporal hunger and Rebekah's manipulation of Isaac's instructions to Esau was context that provided opportunities for the furtherance of Jacob's destiny in line with God's plan and purpose for Jacob. But everyone's destiny will always find context and opportunity for fulfillment.

Joseph's Destiny Clues

Joseph was born the eighth child in his family. He had dreams that pointed to his destiny. He also had unusual favor with his father, who loved him more than his other children (Genesis 37:3)

and made him a tunic of many colors. The tunic was a richly orna-
mented robe and symbolic of Joseph's position in his family. In
addition to these clues, Joseph was thrown into a cistern to be later
pulled up by his brothers. They could have killed him during that
episode, or even handed him a rope to pull himself out. Instead,
by divine providence, he was pulled up and out. These clues fore-
shadowed events that would continue throughout his life. Not only
was he favored by his father, but again by divine providence he had
favor everywhere he went.

Joseph's father had him go check on his brothers and bring
back a report of their welfare, which implicitly pointed to his
leadership as an overseer. In Potiphar's house, in prison, and later
in the kingdom of Egypt, he rose to the top as a leader and was
repeatedly given authority to oversee people and tasks. In the
narrative of Joseph's life we see the repeated mention that "the
Lord was with him" (Genesis 39:2,5,21,23,24), which meant that
God allowed the twists and turns of events to bring Joseph to the
fullness of His purpose for Joseph's life. As we stack these clues
one after the other, we can conclude that our destiny, like those
of Jacob, Joseph, and several others, does not depend on personal
efforts or manipulation but is supernaturally guided to fulfillment
– if God is with us. Fortunately, God desires to be with us, if we
let Him. Time and season will always validate clues on destiny.

Unlike Joseph, Jacob was born fighting for the top position
and would fulfill his destiny by struggling. Through much struggle, he was destined to prevail and fulfill destiny with God's help.
Jacob contended with Esau for what was destined to be his; he
contended with his uncle Laban for his right and prevailed, and he
even contended with God's angel (Genesis 32:24) to receive the
ultimate blessing of his life.

Unlike Jacob, Joseph slept, had dreams, lived right before
God, and merely waited for fulfillment without contending to see
his destiny come to fulfillment. His own destiny was tied to being
a custodian of divine revelations. It is helpful to note that the
legitimate means through which you achieved successes in the
past are foundational clues to how you would primarily achieve
success in the future. It therefore helps to look at trends in your
life's journey for clues on how your future will unfold.

The past is filled with indicators that point to the future. The events of the past, coupled with our interests, proclivities, and feedback from observations by others are instrumental in helping us get on the right path to our destiny. Careful observations can give us signals that will either confirm we are on the right path or caution us if we have derailed from the pathways to our destiny. Whereas warning signs should not be ignored, as they serve to caution us against expending precious time and resources on hopeless initiatives, nudging signs on the other hand help us to stay focused on the right path of hope.

As a young boy growing up, I had the humble privilege of often leading others in most of my endeavors. That was the case in my soccer teams. It was the same in my classrooms from kindergarten through college, just as it was among my friends, peers and ongoing endeavors. I have the natural benefit of being listened to and consider these traits as some of many clues about my destiny.

Another clue was my passion for reading. I had quite a strong interest in reading which was further inspired by my dad, who encouraged me by buying me books that were not necessarily for classroom use, but for general interests. I can still remember vividly, with fascination, several advanced books that others considered too advanced for me at age nine. I read them nonetheless with sufficient clarity and relish some of those narratives even now. I have a great deal of appreciation for the ability of writers to articulate their thoughts in words and to stretch their imaginations. I wanted to be able to do something similar with my imagination.

I am blessed with a wonderful mother who is deeply intelligent but was not given the opportunity of a formal education. When I was a young boy, she would ask me to read the Psalms to her repeatedly. Even though I may not have wanted to because of my sporting hobbies, I nonetheless found it most pleasurable to be asked to read to her. Looking back now I realize that those were pertinent clues pointing to my destiny, particularly as it pertains to my calling as a minister of the gospel of Jesus Christ.

Many who are considered to be successful in their calling showed signs of inherent interest and capabilities in those areas even at tender ages. Some of those who have excelled in engineering, for example, enjoyed building things as children. An outstanding example of this could be found in the lives of the Wright brothers, who invented the first successful airplane. Wilbur and Orville Wright were born to Bishop Milton and Susan Wright. Bishop Wright had the habit of bringing his sons souvenirs from his church travels that included a whirling top toy (a miniature Penaud helicopter in 1878). You could only imagine how excited the Wright brothers were as they flew that first toy! Eighteen years later, together with their passion, their entrepreneurial orientation, and their study of Lilienthal's work and copious research on how birds fly, they were inspired to bring their dream into reality. The Wright brothers' story presents clues of their destiny at the time and season of their opportunity.

Discerning parents have the rare pleasure of identifying clues that point to the destinies of their children. They also have the added advantage of inspiring their children to actualize their destiny. Care must be taken nonetheless to keep an open mind as to the direction they consider that God is leading their children, and not be seen as rushing to conclusions, making irreversible choices for them or limiting their potential.

Some years ago I was talking to my wife about a multiplicity of topics, including politics and life in general as I grew up. From what she heard me say, she randomly said to me, "You should be a writer." Although we laughed about the comment, it resonated with me for quite a while. Again at another occasion, she pointed out that she thought I had a creative mind and often came up with intriguing ideas. She implored me to consider the possibility of putting my ideas into writing because she felt others could be blessed by them. And even though I did not give serious thought to the idea right away, it occasionally struck a serious chord and gentle nudge in me nonetheless. Others have randomly made similar comments, as if to reinforce the clues. What I lacked though was the proper understanding of what they meant, and how to channel some of the God-given capabilities into significance.

Past Mistakes

Life is full of events, decisions, and outcomes that are sometimes within and many times without our control. With the benefit of hindsight, however, we can see that some of our decisions either validated what we later discovered to be our destiny or are pathways toward its fulfillment. Those decisions then became integral aspects of who we became. There were yet other decisions that we felt regrettable. They were nonetheless the best decisions for the time, based on the circumstances and facts at the time. Without the benefit of hindsight, we would most likely make certain decisions over and over again, under the same set of circumstances. Consequently, the outcomes of all the decisions we made in the past or will make in the future could not entirely be within our control. Therefore, you will need to embrace your past with the decisions as well as the outcomes and not brood over what you do not have control over.

Admittedly, there is much we can learn from our past decisions and much we can embrace as well. You cannot change the hand that life deals you, but you can accept it and seek to know how it fits into God's plans for your life in its entirety.

While in prison in Egypt, Joseph may have had moments in which he reflected on his past and regretted what he thought were mistakes. He may have felt that he made a mistake to have shared his dreams with his brothers. While living in the heat of the outcome of seemingly poor choices that we made, there is the tendency to have regrets. However, when we read the narrative of Joseph's life in its entirety, it is clear that his actions fit perfectly with God's overall plan for his life and brought him closer to the fulfillment of his destiny. Had he not shared his dreams, they would not have plotted to kill him and subsequently sold him as a slave. And if they had not sold him as a slave, he certainly would not have had the chance of getting into Egypt, nor would he have gone through the preparation needed to excel in the palace that he received while in Potiphar's house and later in prison. He probably also regretted telling Pharaoh's jailed chief cupbearer the interpretation to his dream, particularly when he later forgot to put in word for Joseph to Pharaoh, after his restoration, as promised (Genesis 40:23).

It is obvious that the seeming mistakes made by Jacob, Joseph, Moses, and others we have studied did not prevent the fulfillment of their destinies. We therefore have the comfort of history that those decisions we thought were mistakes will not prevent the fulfillment of our destinies. We need to accept the events that have transpired in our past and move forward to our future.

In God's Presence

In the presence of God, destinies are made. Rather than being afraid of making mistakes or dwelling on thoughts of things you could have done differently, focus your attention on being in God's presence and let Him guide your steps and lead you on the right paths to your destiny. Saul, in the Acts of the Apostles (later known as Paul), was transformed when he came into the presence of God. Moses came into God's presence and was forever changed.

Everyone that encounters God and allows Him to lead him will inevitably fulfill destiny. You are positioning yourself for destiny when you allow God to direct your steps in obedience to what He created you to be. In God's presence, your past missteps are corrected and turned to blessings. It is in having a right relationship with God that all things work together for your good (Romans 8:28). Moses, Jacob, Paul, and many others with shaky pasts experienced firsthand the ability and willingness of God to utilize their imperfections and reconfigure their lives in order to help them fulfill their destinies.

Chapter exercise:

1. Ask your parents or guardians about any credible revelations, prophesies or insightful clues they may have about your destiny.

2. Jot down clues from your past that are indicative of where you are heading, or things you should be doing now or in the future.

    a. What success indicators are keyed into your past clues?

    b. Are there traits such as being contentious like Jacob that you should pursue?

    c. Are there special gifts, such as "revelation" (as with Joseph), that you need to develop?

d. Are there proclivities, such as defending the weak (as with Moses), that you need to embrace?

e. What passions, interests, and inclinations gave you success in the past that you need to further exploit?

Chapter Eleven:

God and People Focused

"'You shall love the LORD your God with all your heart, with all your soul, with all your strength, and with all your mind,' and 'your neighbor as yourself.'"
– Luke 10:27

"If you want one year of prosperity, grow grain. If you want ten years of prosperity, grow trees. If you want one hundred years of prosperity, grow people."
– Chinese Proverb

People matter! It is amazing how much emphasis many cultures in the world place on self-actualization and acquisition of material possessions for personal consumption. It is ridiculous how much trampling we see in the bid to get ahead of others. How about the employee that makes his colleagues look bad in order to get ahead of them in the organizational hierarchy? How about the businessperson that willfully pushes unsafe products to the market to maximize profit? Consider the fraudsters and tricksters who would raise people's hopes when there really are no hopes?

People who have left lasting legacies on the sands of time have been mostly selfless, giving up personal gains for the benefit of others. They are those whose achievements and contributions impact their generation and their community beyond their lifetimes. They are leaders whose performance and achievements and the resulting legacies were centered on people. They did not take advantage of people but were vulnerable instead and sometimes allowed themselves to be taken advantage of unknowingly.

Jesus came to fulfill a destiny centered on people. In Matthew

4 Jesus was tempted by Satan in the wilderness on three distinctive levels. First, He was tempted in the area of food, similar to Esau, who forfeited his birthright because of food, and Isaac, who could not tame his appetite and needed some well-cooked game before blessing his son. Secondly, He was faced with the temptation to act in arrogance. And thirdly, He was tempted to accept the kingdoms of the world and its glory. He did not succumb to any of the three. He overcame Satan by the Word of God. He knew the purpose of His coming to earth and refused to compromise it on any ground.

When we compromise our destiny because of the means of our livelihood, we run into the danger of quashing it. When, as was the case with Satan's second temptation of Jesus, we are tempted in the area of pride and arrogance, it behooves us to stay humble under the mighty and sustaining hand of God through confession of and obedience to God's Word as Jesus did, or else we will thwart God's plan and be derailed from fulfilling our destiny. We also cannot allow fame, wealth, power, prestige, and influence of this world to trip us, just as Jesus did not. Those whose focus is on fulfilling their destiny must not subject themselves to the lust of the flesh, the lust of the eyes, and the pride of life, which are not godly but worldly (1 John 2:16). We cannot serve God and mammon (Matthew 6:24).

I am particularly grateful that Jesus focused wholly on His purpose to redeem mankind from sin and was determined to fulfill it. That was His destiny – humankind's redemption. Every aspect of Jesus' ministry focused on people. At the cross, while in agonizing pain, Jesus took the time to say to John: "Behold your mother" (John 19:27). After His resurrection, He could have rushed back to heaven to be seated in glory at the right hand of God the Father, yet He took His time to ensure that people were taken care of. He said to Peter, if you love Me, "feed my sheep" (John 21:16). The Great Commission to His disciples after His resurrection, "go into all the world and preach the gospel" (Mark 16:15), was also about helping people. Jesus' entire life was devoted to people.

People that make lasting differences are those who recognize that their destiny involves impacting the lives of others. Whatever your vocation might be, your destiny is never about you. It is God that gives dreams, callings, and missions, and they are greater than the individual. Your destiny revolves around people. After God had introduced Himself to Moses, He proceeded to introduce Moses' mission. It was not about Moses. Notice the focus of the mission – people: "And the LORD said: I have surely seen the oppression of My *people* who are in Egypt, and have heard their cry because of their taskmasters, for I know their sorrows" (Exodus 3:7).

At the core of your destiny is a mandate to meet people's needs: orphans, poor, sick, oppressed, weak, abandoned, and homeless people. God blessed Abraham to be a blessing and not to live for himself. God raised Gideon as a judge to address the problem facing his people Israel. That is the way God works in matters of destiny. That is the same way He is working with you. You have something to offer. True fulfillment is found in being a blessing to others. Your destiny involves reaching out and being a blessing to your world, starting with your local community in the area God has called you.

God opens doors for greater impact and influence to those who bless others. In his letter to the generous disciples at Corinth that were poised to help others, Paul prayed a revelatory prayer: "Now may He who supplies seed to the sower, and bread for food, supply and multiply the seed you have sown and increase the fruits of your righteousness" (2 Corinthians 9:10). The substance with which you bless others is a privilege that comes from God. As you release that into the lives of others, God multiples the substance back to you and gives you an increased capacity to do more.

You should ask yourself these questions: What are the needs of people that I have a passion toward meeting? How can I begin to meet those needs today? You may not be able to solve the problems facing the entire world, no one individual can, but you can begin to meet the need of one person at a time, as God gives you opportunity. The poor widow of Zarephath (1 Kings 17) gave water and used up her last flour and oil to feed Elijah in a selfless act, and her destiny was preserved. We read about her reward in 1 Kings 17:14: "For thus says the LORD God of Israel: 'The bin of flour shall not be used up, nor shall the jar of oil run dry, until the day the LORD sends rain on the earth.'" Her capacity was increased by God, while her destiny and that of her son were preserved.

Jesus said in Luke 14:13-14, "But when you give a feast, invite the poor, the maimed, the lame, the blind. And you will be blessed, because they cannot repay you; for you shall be repaid at the resurrection of the just." Here we find a commandment accompanied by reward (*you will be blessed*). Unfortunately, people are inclined to be selfish, self-centered, and to look down on the less privileged. God's kingdom does not work that way, as God is always looking for selfless people who would step up to bless others. When God finds such people, He positions them and increases their capacity to be of further blessing. Proverbs 19:17 says: "He who has pity on the poor lends to the LORD, and He will pay back what he has given."

God's primary interest is people, and He uses people to bless other people. He delights in seeing you become a blessing to people, particularly those that are less privileged around you. You must already know that all around you are victims of injustice, the poor, the oppressed, and the weak. You have the opportunity to make a difference as you bless such people in an area that aligns with your interest and passion. That is what fulfilling your destiny is ultimately about – meeting the needs of people!

Helping others does not necessarily have to be in giving away cash. A researcher with the passion or interest to help alcoholics can commence a research to find a solution to the problem primarily to help victims, rather than be driven by profit-making motives. A movie producer may produce movies that shed light on the problem of abandoned and neglected children worldwide, thereby creating awareness for others with interest and ability to adopt or help in other ways. The key is to identify your passion and interest as they relate to the needs out there, and then take steps to partake in the solution. As you embrace the problems facing people, God marks you for something greater than yourself.

For Christians who are not directly involved with ministry (i.e. functioning in the apostolic, pastoral, evangelistic, prophetic, and/or teaching office) as stated in Ephesians 4:11, there should be a deliberate act of equipping for good works so they can be a blessing to others, just as Jesus was (Acts 10:38). If you are in the marketplace (professional, businessperson, etc.) you should be kingdom-minded (Matthew 6:33) and live the lifestyle that puts God's will and agenda above yours. Walk the opportune path that blesses others instead of the loud and shiny road of self-centeredness. Remember that it is God who gives you the power to get wealth in order to be a blessing. Paul reaffirms in 1 Corinthians 4:7: "For who makes you differ from another? And what do you have that you did not receive? Now if you did indeed receive it, why do you boast as if you had not received it?" It is only in God and through His supernatural provision that we can realize our true destiny.

God wants you to be comfortable but not to hoard wealth, while overlooking those in need. If done right, sharing your blessings with others could be an effective expression of God's love and a potentially powerful way to share the gospel of Jesus with them. Paul said in Ephesians 4:28: "Let him who stole steal no longer, but rather let him labor, working with his hands what is good, that he may have something to give him who has need." Note that Paul's admonition does not stop at asking thieves (including the greedy and selfish) not to steal anymore, but also encourages them to work so they can be of help to the needy.

Selflessness, like pure and undefiled religion, is "to visit orphans and widows in their trouble, and to keep oneself unspotted from the world" (James 1:27). It is not amassing wealth for oneself and turning a blind eye to the needy. It is not building barricades to keep the poor and less privileged away. It is serving the unprivileged, as Jesus did. Jesus' mission statement was: "The Spirit of the LORD is upon Me, Because He has anointed Me *to preach the gospel to the poor; He has sent Me to heal the brokenhearted, to proclaim liberty to the captives and recovery of sight to the blind, to set at liberty those who are oppressed*" (Luke 4:18). If we choose to follow His example and become like Jesus, then our mission should resemble His.

God is very much interested in leading us and getting us to our destiny and ultimately to our eternal destination with Him in heaven. Satan can frustrate our destiny and lead us to the wrong destination, which is hell. Satan has always had a contrary agenda from God's. In a derailed destiny, you will find yourself pulled in different directions and tempted to self-gratify, the consequence of which is often expressed in depression, frustration, confusion, failure, hopelessness, and the like. Derailed destiny leaves an aching void in the heart and in the soul. For instance, a detour from the path God has laid out for you for, say, financial and material gains will always end up in dissatisfaction and the feeling of frustration, simply because money and stuff do not satisfy God-given yearnings of the soul.

The Bible states in Romans 8:29 that God "foreknew and predestined" us. We were created with a predestination and purpose in God's mind and are prompted to do His good pleasures. Philippians 2:13 says that "for it is God who works in you both to will and to do for His good pleasure." God invites us to fulfill our destiny by giving us specific desires and interests. Unless we embrace His invitation and travel the paths He calls us to walk, fulfillment of those callings might prove elusive.

Knowing God

As earlier stated, listening to and hearing from God requires discernment. Filtering out the voice of the enemy is like perfecting the art of tuning into the right radio frequency. Jesus' followers will know His voice, just as the sheep knows the voice of its shepherd because of intimacy – the time spent together with the shepherd. Children know the voice of their parents or guardians with whom they spend time together. I know the voice of my father because of the time I have spent with him. I know the peculiar pitch of his voice and his demeanor. I also know what he can or cannot say based on known principles and values about him. You must know God enough to know His voice, His values, His character, and His expectations. You should be able to discern what God is truly saying by aligning with His Word. We should be able to say with confidence that a particular direction in which we are being led is in consonance with where our heavenly Father is leading us.

Knowing God entails spending time with Him. Our time in God's presence allows us to speak with Him and affords Him the reciprocity of speaking with us. It is in His presence that our steps are guided aright. It is in His presence that our decisions get subjected to God's purpose for our life. It is there that our mistakes, though with potential devastation, get beautifully redirected to fit into God's plans through divine orchestration – as Romans 8:28 attests, toward fulfilling our destiny. That's where He shepherds us and leads us in the path leading to the destiny He prepared for us. It is there that we understand His will and agenda for our lives. It is in His presence that we can experience what Prophet Isaiah attests (Isaiah 30:21) to: "Your ears shall hear a word behind you, saying, 'This is the way, walk in it,' whenever you turn to the right hand or whenever you turn to the left." You can only hear from such close proximity as a result of intimacy!

Also see Psalm 81:13, Jeremiah 10:23, and Isaiah 8:11.

Loving and Hearing God

"And you shall love the LORD your God with all your heart, with all your soul, with all your mind, and with all your strength. This is the first commandment" (Mark 12:30). You do not value what you do not appreciate, and you're unlikely to pursue what you don't appreciate or value. Here is how David the psalmist and second king of Israel puts it: "Delight yourself in the LORD and He will give you the desires of your heart. Commit your way to the LORD; trust in Him and He will do this: He will make your righteousness shine like the dawn, the justice of your cause like the noonday sun" (Psalm 37:4-6).

Loving God and developing a healthy relationship with Him are paramount to fulfilling our destiny. Our ultimate objective is to give God glory. The extent to which we maximize the glory we render to God is directly proportional to our ability to maximize our potential in fulfilling His purpose for our lives. In order to know His purpose for our lives and to navigate the destiny paths God has mapped out for us, we need to have the capability to receive instructions from Him. That is the true expression of our love for God.

Hearing God is vitally important. Everyone that God calls, He also leads to fulfill his destiny; but no one could be led by God who will not first hear from Him. Like Abraham, Moses, Gideon, Saul, David, Jeremiah, and other great men and women in the Bible, you do not truly begin your journey until you begin hearing from God. Hearing God begins with tuning into the frequency through God's channel of communication. Obviously, if you cannot hear Him, you do not stand a chance of obeying Him.

Abraham would never have commenced his journey to his destiny if he had not heard God's instructions in Genesis 12:1. But when God said "Get out of your country, from your family and from your father's house, to a land that I will show you..." he was willing to identify with the will of God – in obedience. Here was Abraham's expression of love for God. It was also God's expression of commitment to Abraham as He took responsibility for leading Abraham through the pathways to the fulfillment of his destiny.

Sticking with God in love means that we will stay the course, irrespective of what comes our way. Abraham made mistakes along the way when he took his eyes off course and his ears off hearing God. He began to trust in his own understanding. He went in to Hagar, and Ishmael was born, the distraction of which was to create pain and frustration in his family. Whereas the Word of God admonishes us: "Trust in the LORD with all your heart, and lean not on your own understanding; in all your ways acknowledge Him, and He shall direct your paths" (Proverbs 3:5-6).

Absolute trust emanates from unwavering and undisguised love. Moses, David, and Paul, for example, fulfilled their destinies for as long as they accorded God prominence in their lives. The love of God must precede true success or it (success) soon becomes short-lived. Until God revealed His purpose and gave these faith-worthies the clearance to proceed they would not, because they loved God. A life of misery and insignificance awaits anyone who will start their journey to destiny without due consideration to the love for God.

Love God with all the essence of your being, and build up your relationship with Him through disciplines that include praying, studying the Bible, and fellowshipping with other believers. The fulfillment of destiny involves staying connected with God, who does the leading along our pathways, and having an appreciation for the people God leads us to serve in various capacities.

God, People, and Predestination

Romans 8:28-29 says that "all things work together for good to those who love God, to those who are the called according to His purpose. For whom He foreknew, He also predestined to be conformed to the image of His Son that He might be the firstborn among many brethren." Isn't it wonderful that God created, foreknew, and predestined us to be conformed to the image of His Son? It certainly must be comforting to know that He did all that in accordance to His purpose. Any deliberate derailment from this purpose must therefore be a deviation from God's foreknowledge and predestination.

Yet the question commonly asked continues to be the one on how we can know what our destiny is. To discover and fulfill our destiny, we must involve God. We must seek Him and ask Him with an open and sincere heart. It is like asking someone along our path the way to a destination with a genuine readiness to hear from and follow the person who knows. Our God knows the way and will point us to the right direction.

Many have trod the paths to wealth, possessions, and fame only to discover much too late that they are devoid of fulfillment of their destiny. They arrived at the fame station and obtained influence but missed the mark of their calling. There is nothing wrong with wealth and fame. Neither is there anything wrong with influence and power, as long as they are seen as means of fulfilling God's purposes for our lives. Apart from God, those pursuits are baseless, ephemeral, and inconsequential. It is only with God's guidance that we discover and walk the paths of our destiny to fulfillment.

What therefore is a fulfilled life like? We have an example in the person of God's Son, Jesus. We are told that being in the form of man, He identified His destiny and focused on fulfilling it. In His journey, He refused to be derailed by the temptation to grab onto influence, power, and worldly wealth. Instead He focused on fulfilling the Father's will for His life. We also need to embrace the attitude, image, and likeness of Jesus Christ. We need to focus on fulfilling the purpose of God's call upon our lives.

A good yardstick to measure our progress toward attaining our destiny is our resemblance to Jesus Christ's mandate. We are told in Acts 10:38 "how God anointed Jesus of Nazareth with the Holy Spirit and with power, who went about doing good and healing all who were oppressed by the devil, for God was with Him." The closer we are in resemblance to Him, the more confident we become that we are on the right path. On the other hand, the less resemblance we have to Him, the farther away from our destiny we become and, regrettably, the more frustrated, distressed, and disappointed we also are.

If you are succeeding in your resemblance to the image and likeness of Jesus, congratulations! Continue to close the gap. If however you feel the struggle and consider that you do not yet look like Jesus in doing what God wants you to do, don't be discouraged. God is gracious and full of love and will draw you closer if you draw closer to Him. Spend time with God in prayer, in the study of His Word, and fellowship with people of like mind in Christ. Before long you'll begin to see that you are being conformed to the desired image of Jesus Christ.

Predestination as in Romans 8:28-29 speaks to those that love God (or choose to love God) and should not be misunderstood to mean that

God already chose those on whom He will bestow salvation, success, and good fortune exclusively. The Bible reveals that God is "not willing that any should perish but that all should come to repentance" (2 Peter 3:9) and "For God so loved the world that He gave His only begotten Son, that <u>whoever</u> believes in Him should not perish but have everlasting life" (John 3:16). God is not bias. He welcomes everyone who chooses to turn away from sin to be part of His family.

Choices and Baggage

Salvation is a choice, and the decision to follow Jesus has never been by compulsion. Everyone has free will. You have a role to play in determining the trajectory of your destiny by your decision to accept or reject God's Son, Jesus, into your life. In John 3:16, we see that God so loved the world and gave His only begotten Son as a sacrifice so that whoever (no exception) chooses to believe and accept Him will not perish (or die an unfulfilled life that is followed by judgment) but will have a wholesome, fulfilled life that will continue into eternity. The choice of which path we follow is ours. And even when we follow the path of life that Jesus has prepared for us before time, it is also a matter of choice how we travel the path.

Anyone may choose to travel the path of life lightly or with unnecessary and varying weight of baggage. In life, people's baggage often includes a mix of bad habits, negative thinking, and attitudes, bitterness, unforgiveness, bad company, lust, anger, cruelty, hatred, and many more or all of them. Unnecessary baggage weighs us down and threatens our ability to arrive at our destination, as and when we should. Hebrews 12:1 admonishes "let us lay aside every weight and the sin which so easily ensnares us, and let us run with endurance the race that is set before us."

Baggage has significant impact on our life's journey. I have traveled quite a bit over the years and realize from experience that the more baggage I bring along, the more stressed and bugged down I feel. However, the less baggage I bring along, the more pleasant and agile my travel is. The same principles apply with life. How you travel on the pathways to destiny matters. Travel light and let go of unnecessary baggage and you will arrive sooner than later.

Your choices will directly determine the quality of life you live on earth. Be careful enough to ponder the fact that your life does not consist of the abundance of things you possess (Luke 12:15), but rather in the things that glorify and please God (Matthew 6:33).

An example of God's universal love toward mankind can be seen in the lives of Jacob and Esau. While God decided to make Jacob a greater nation, it must be well understood that He did not start off with disdain for Esau as some have believed. He simply revealed to Rachel that: "Two nations are in your womb, two peoples shall be separated from your body; one people shall be stronger than the other, and the older shall serve the younger" (Genesis 25:23). In itself, it wasn't a bad arrangement. This foreshadows how things will unravel in the kingdom of God, in which the last will be first and the humble exalted above the proud. Jesus reiterated the need for His disciples to humble themselves. In Malachi 1:3 God spoke of His hatred for Esau in response to his foolish choice and disregard for his chronology. God spoke in the past tense, looking back at what transpired in the lives of two brothers who made different choices with respect to their inheritance. God loved Jacob's enthusiasm to fulfill His destiny, and blessed him. On the other hand, He hated Esau's carelessness and his corresponding poor choices that took him further away from the fulfillment of his destiny. Rather than repent of his sin and return to the God of his fathers (Abraham and Isaac), he decided on a path that took him further away from God and his destiny by marrying the Hittite and Canaanite women. Esau's decisions grieved his parents (Genesis 26:34-35). His choices were in direct defiance and opposition to God's law.

Imagine that God expects man to not live by bread alone. Esau chose to live by bread when he betrayed his destiny for a morsel of pottage. Secondly, God expects honor to be given to our father and mother. Esau deliberately married foreign women and made life bitter for his parents (Isaac and Rebekah). Esau seemingly lived an independent and rebellious life, contrary to the desire of God and his parents in the very important decision of marriage. Esau set the stage for himself to be derailed from his destiny by his choices, his permissive lifestyle, and his dishonor for his parents. The consequences were tortuous and long-lasting, ending with the loss of the all-important blessing of the firstborn, which though he cried for bitterly he did not receive (Genesis 27:22-37, Hebrews 12:15-17).

While the events surrounding Rebekah's manipulation cannot be undermined, God had destined both Esau and Jacob to be blessed, except that Jacob would be greater. Jacob made choices and walked the path that made it possible for him to fulfill his destiny, including listening to his parents' counsel (certainly his mother's). That was the path of parental counsel that helped Jacob realize the blessing that Esau rejected to his detriment. Choices will either bring you closer to or further from your destiny. Watch your choices and be careful to have them guarded and directed toward God's will.

Jacob's parting blessings on his sons as recorded in Genesis 49 is very compelling. We are able to catch a glimpse of the destinies of a few of his sons: Reuben his firstborn should have excelled in honor and power, but he fell short of attaining his destiny because of poor choices. He was said to lack self-control, as he chose to sleep with his old father's wife (Genesis 49:4). Simeon and Levi were characterized by anger and cruelty that truncated their destinies (Genesis 49:5-7). Judah, because of right choices, received a great inheritance of blessing from Jacob his father, in the place where his three elder brothers failed. He refused to carry along with him similar baggage that the three elder brothers carried.

Character Traits

Every Christian needs to be reminded that his choices bear a perfect reflection of his character. We all need to pay closer attention to our character. A thorough study of the life of Joseph and his brothers reveals character traits with significant implications to their destinies. Have you discovered your character traits? Take a moment to jot them down. Could you identify character traits that are capable of aborting your destiny? Would you deal with them before they deal with you? Genesis 4:6-7 says, "So the LORD said to Cain, 'Why are you angry? And why has your countenance fallen? If you do well, will you not be accepted? And if you do not do well, sin lies at the door. And its desire is for you, but you should rule over it.'" God brought the destiny-aborting baggage of anger to Cain's attention and asked him to overcome it. He also informed Cain that if he made the right choices by doing well like his brother Abel, he would likewise be accepted. God made it clear that Cain needed to master sin and put his anger, which led him to sin, under control, otherwise

144

he stood the danger of being mastered and enslaved by sin.

Cain's destiny was derailed because he did not heed God's warning concerning his baggage and choices. Similar to Cain in the matter of unchecked anger was Moses, who accomplished great things in the deliverance of Israel from the enslaving hands of Egypt's Pharaoh, but he failed to enter the Promised Land. In his anger and lack of self-control, he killed an Egyptian (Exodus 2:12). Later, still with unchecked anger, he smashed the tablets containing the Ten Commandments he had received from God (Exodus 32:19). In Numbers 20:8 God instructed him to speak to the rock. Again in anger, he struck the rock (Numbers 20:11). There is nothing in the Scriptures that indicate he could not have entered the Promised Land if he had bridled this monstrous trait – anger!

Honor

In an era of moral decline such as we have, honor is a critical success factor that is often overlooked. With the evolution of societies, people have become increasingly detached from one another. Some children would rather live far from parents, and we continue to have higher levels of independence than the generations before us. The "race to the top" and other competitive philosophies have caused many to adopt the mindset of "the end justifying the means." Honor has been desecrated, as it were. There is an unhealthy sense of disregard like never before imagined for parents, elders, and, sadly enough, for strategic destiny helpers that God has placed along our pathways. Left unchecked, these potential blind spots can be lethally detrimental to our ability to fulfill destiny.

In Leviticus 19:32 God enjoins the younger: "You shall rise before the gray headed and honor the presence of an old man, and fear your God: I am the LORD." Paul's writing in Ephesians 6:2 exhorts us to: "Honor your father and mother, which is the first commandment with promise." Jesus, in rebuking those that failed to honor their elders, said in Matthew 15:6 that dishonoring one's father and mother invalidates God's Word in the life of the perpetrator. Those to be honored as fathers and mothers include older men and women (1 Timothy 5:1-3) as well as those that assume parental roles and oversight over us, among whom are spiritual parents, parents in-law, foster parents, and mentors.

A contemporary example of honoring our fathers and mothers came during the 2008 presidential election when Jeremiah Wright, then pastor to presidential hopeful Barack Obama, made several controversial remarks about the United States and his "spiritual son," Barack Obama. In the midst of the controversy, and at a time when many in his position would distance themselves from a seemingly divisive figure for the sake of winning political office, Barack Obama continued to honor this spiritual father and elder and did not speak ill of him in the media (or otherwise, as far as I am aware). Though he did not seem to identify with Jeremiah Wright's controversial views, Obama continued to associate with him and to honor him nonetheless.

God's commandment in Exodus 20:12 says: "honor your father and your mother, that your days may be long upon the land which the LORD your God is giving you."

Notice that God places no condition for honoring our parents. It's irrelevant whether they deserve it or not. We are expected to give them honor so that our days might be long in the land. To die before one's predestined time is to shorten life's journey, not realizing or optimizing one's potential in fulfilling destiny. It is unfortunate to be prematurely removed from the land God gives – whether it is in the form of business, status, and authority or even a leadership position. It pleases God when you honor your parents, those assuming parental roles in your life, leaders, and the elderly (see 1 Peter 2:17, 1 Timothy 6:1, Ephesians 6:1-3, Proverbs 30:17, Proverbs 20:20). Honor is due to our elders, and those who hold their elders contemptuously do so to their eternal hurt.

Chapter questions:
1. What are your character traits? Take a moment to jot them down.

2. Could you identify those character traits that are capable of aborting your destiny? Would you commit to addressing them?

3. What kinds of choices are you prone to making?

4. How would you describe your walk/relationship with God? What adjustments can you make to draw closer to Him?

Chapter Twelve:

Destiny Busters

"The thief does not come except to steal, and to kill, and to destroy. I have come that they may have life, and that they may have it more abundantly."
– John 10:10

"Watch your thoughts, for they become words. Watch your words, for they become actions. Watch your actions, for they become habits. Watch your habits, for they become character. Watch your character, for it becomes your destiny."
– Unknown

A traveler on the pathways to destiny must be aware of the landmarks and signposts along the way. There is no one straight, smooth, predestined path to fulfillment. Landmarks or signs may be positive or negative, beneficial or detrimental, encouraging or discouraging, and motivating or crippling.

Fear and Discouragement

While there are a number of destiny busters that include procrastination, negative words, doubt, unbelief, association with negative people, and so on, *fear* and *discouragement* are two major destiny busters. They often creep into our path at major life intersections in subtle ways. How we address them determines our ability to advance toward our destiny, get stuck, or retreat. When faced with fear, many people remain static and never venture forward in life. Such people minimize or stifle their potential. Traveling the path of least resistance could similarly be a dangerous temptation when yielded to.

Those that have succeeded to realize their destinies have been people who faced their destiny head-on. They did not entertain fear and discouragement because they realized their crippling effects.

Your main hope toward reaching your destiny is to forge ahead, irrespective of threatening fear and discouragement that you face along the way, and regardless of how insurmountable the mountain appears.

I enjoy driving long distances and have a preference for late-night driving because the roads are relatively much freer at night than at day. I always hope I won't run into deer as I travel through wooded areas. I remember a particular trip from Boston to Pennsylvania in the winter in which I noticed several signs warning about deer crossing. Though I have been fortunate not to run into any deer, I understand that when deer are crossing the highway at nighttime and see the light of a fast-approaching vehicle, they freeze and stand still. They get stuck, stand still, and increase the probability of getting hit (and causing damage to the automobile). Though the deer is also on a journey to some desired destination, a deer that stops in the middle of the road due to fear will be hit by a fast-moving automobile and will very likely die on the spot. Should the deer retreat, it may live but never reach its destination at the desired time – assuming time was of the essence in the animal kingdom.

One may think of it as a mere life event, or a function of chance or fate. The deer has a role to play in the outcome of its life as external factors creep up. The deer has a much greater chance of survival if it continues to run across the road, irrespective of the unexpected snag along the way, than if it stands still or attempts to retreat. By stopping and allowing fear and discouragement of undesired problems to stop it in its path, it is exposed to death and derailment from its destination. So it is with humans.

Fear and discouragement have devastating and crippling effects on us if we do not conquer them by moving forward. Untamed fear and discouragement can stop you from fulfilling your destiny. Where there is fear and discouragement, an individual has difficulty taking on a new project, pursuing promising career opportunities, starting a ministry, or embarking on a new venture. Fear and discouragement keep one grounded and stuck even when abundant opportunities beckon. The fact remains that no mountain is insurmountable where there is a will. If you allow fear in your life, it will rob you of the will to make attempts at scaling over hurdles. It will keep you at the same spot, lingering in indecision and unable to get to your finish line.

Consider the intelligence efforts made by Israel ahead of their possessing Canaan in Numbers 14. Ten of the twelve spies sent were filled with fear and discouragement. When they looked at the land, they saw good things and desired them, but when they looked at the dwellers on the land, they saw giants and developed fear and discouragement. To the ten men, God's Promised Land seemed impossible to attain. They did not get to their destination because they died in the wilderness. To the two others (Joshua and Caleb), who against fear had faith and against discouragement had unwavering courage, God granted grace to fulfill their destinies and enter the land flowing with milk and honey because they saw differently – by faith.

Many still fall today in the wilderness of their lives because of fear and discouragement. Joshua and Caleb believed that they could overcome the Canaanite inhabitants, notwithstanding their size and strength. They had a "can do" attitude that subdued fear and discouragement: an attitude that will always help in our journey to fulfilling destiny.

Notice also in 1 Samuel 17 that when the giant Goliath of the Philistines challenged the Israelites with intimidating tactics, they were crippled with fear and discouragement. Israel was intimated for forty days till they had to give up the fight. We are told that "When the Israelites saw the man, they all ran from him in great fear." Fear crippled Israel until the bold, courageous young man David arrived. As a young shepherd, David had learned to conquer fear and discouragement. What's more, he was certain that the "uncircumcised" Goliath could not withstand him, who had experience overcoming the lion and the bear with God's help. He was convinced that Goliath's intimidation was nothing in the face of faith. He had no doubt that Goliath would also fall by his hands with God's help. Sure enough, Goliath fell by David's hands.

In order to fulfill your destiny, it is imperative that you realize you are unique just as your destiny is. Step away from the negative influences of the crowd, particularly when they tend toward fear and discouragement. Embrace opportunities as well as challenges along your pathways to destiny with boldness, courage, and faith like David did. You must dare to be distinct and step away from the status quo. David went on to defeat Goliath and stepped further into the fulfillment of his destiny. Goliath's defeat was much easier than anyone anticipated. Fear and discouragement are notorious for magnifying the challenges of life.

When you reflect on some of your major accomplishments in life, you may find that many of them involved undertakings that were seemingly unattainable or difficult. But you skipped through them anyway. Those were the preparations for the challenges you are now faced with, or that you will face in the future. The fact is that when the challenges came, you did not cower in fear and discouragement under them. You set your heart to doing what you had to do and you did them – in faith.

Seeing situations from the perspective of fear and discouragement limits the drive to commence or accomplish the task ahead. It is best to see from God's limitless perspective. View your calling and assignment as a project and God as your project owner. He has vested interest in the project's success for His greater glory. He created you and predestined you and will make all things work together for your good. And if you would walk the paths He has predetermined for you, fear and discouragement will have no power over you, because God will ensure that you succeed anyway.

Remember, God's plans for your life come in dreams and passions that are bigger than you, therefore they require His power and ability to bring them to fruition. You are essentially a vessel through which great and noble plans are accomplished. If Martin Luther King Jr. were alive today, he would probably be awestruck to see how much God could do through a life that is completely yielded to Him. Martin Luther King Jr., as we all know, worked hard and played out his God-assigned role during the days of the American Civil Rights movement. He had a dream, followed his passion, and refused to entertain fear and discouragement. That dream has come to pass. Not just because a black man was elected president of the United States forty-four years later, but because several others had stepped into leadership positions as governors, senators, congressmen, mayors, secretaries of state, and more.

Similarly, Nelson Mandela of South Africa, Mahatma Gandhi of India, and several others accomplished their dreams as they fought boldly and courageously and against all odds, and they have gone down in the annals of history as fulfilling their destinies. Dreams remain only mental imagery unless they are acted upon by the dreamer and blessed by God – the dream giver.

Excuses

Excuses are hindrances that inhibit one's ability to fulfill destiny. Read Exodus 3 and you will see how Moses, for example, was armed with excuses when God called him to travel the path that would lead to his great destiny. In the wilderness he heard the call of God asking for him to become His ambassador to Egypt. He assured Moses that He would go with him and that He had made full provision, yet Moses was afraid and felt inadequate. Moses used his natural deficiencies as excuses not to go the direction God wanted for him. His excuses included the fact that he was naturally ineloquent and did not seem to have what it would take to stand before Pharaoh and demand the end to Israel's enslavement.

In Exodus 6:28-30 Moses claimed to be of *"uncircumcised lips"* and concluded that Pharaoh would not listen to him. God, in His tender mercies, had to convince Moses that "I have made you as God to Pharaoh, and Aaron your brother will be your prophet" (Exodus 7:1). His excuses of fear, doubt, unbelief, and insecurity were gone when he believed God. He summed up courage and took the step of faith to do what he was called to do.

As God calls you to greatness, do not make excuses of one inadequacy or the other. God uses imperfect people and has your weaknesses covered, irrespective of whether they are real or perceived. Arise by faith and report for duty before God; obey, move forward with courage, and you are sure to fulfill your destiny.

Complacency

Complacency is a silent destiny killer that imposes itself on its victim without obvious threat. It is that feeling of contentment or self-satisfaction, especially in the face of daunting danger, trouble, or controversy. It shows up when you have somewhat attained and gives an exaggerated sense of accomplishment in the middle of a journey with fractional success, even though you know there is still much ground to cover.

Throughout history in general, and the Bible in particular, we see people who came short of their destinies because of complacency. Complacency makes people give up on God's plans for their lives. It suppresses one's ability to dream and aspire for more in life. It tends toward mediocrity. You can identify complacency when you begin to rationalize or fabricate excuses as to why you cannot accomplish more in life. You must deal with it and abhor it.

It is no doubt rewarding to stop periodically to acknowledge and celebrate progress. What is not acceptable is to rest on one's oars as if the journey had ended and all opportunities are retired. We must exercise great care to guard against subtle complacency. We cannot afford to let our guards down, relent, or give up. Instead, we must keep striving. We must keep advancing and keep breaking new ground. We must discern our next assignments and pursue them with fervor. As long as we live, there will always be the next assignment and a mission to be accomplished. Go for it!

God expects everyone to be ever increasing, not staying stagnant at the same spot. He created man to be fruitful and to multiply (Genesis 1:28). When we cease to bear fruit and multiply, we become complacent. Soon, if we do not take corrective actions, we will begin to decline and eventually die. You should be constantly on the move toward new altitudes. The apostle Paul was a good example of a success story. He was never complacent. As we read in his epistles (Philippians 3:7-14), against all odds, even in chains, he pressed forward and accomplished great things for God's kingdom.

While writing this book, my eight-year-old daughter shared an insight that I thought is quite profound. She said, "Your destiny is [uniquely] yours, so you have to discover it." What an amazing revelation! Everyone's destiny does not get dropped on his lap. Each of us has to seek it out. This truth applies similarly to those born with privileged positions as well as those not so privileged. A prince, princess, king, or priest with no distinctive destiny is just a mere human with nothing to show for living. Your destiny is what sets you apart from the rest, and you have to search it out in order to fulfill it. Proverbs 25:2 says that "it is the glory of God to conceal a matter, but the honor of kings to search out a matter." As Christians, we are all kings according to Revelation 5:10.

If Jacob had chosen to remain in Padan Aram, he would have remained frustrated and eventually died with his destiny unfulfilled like his grandfather, Terah, who set out for the land of Canaan but settled in Haran instead, not reaching his destination and not accomplishing his destiny. Instead, Jacob stepped out against the fear of Esau to seek out his destiny and fulfill it. Have you cared to discover what your destiny is? Are you stepping out in faith toward accomplishing it?

Another helpful consideration is the story of Esther and Mordecai (Esther's cousin) contained in the book of Esther chapters 1-10. Esther, having become the queen, could have been complacent, keeping to herself and not considering the fate of the Jews, who were threatened with death by the influential Haman. But she took action and saved both her generation as well as generations unborn that would have been annihilated (Esther 3:6) had Haman's plot succeeded. Mordecai faced a powerful establishment. He also had the choice of being complacent when Bigthana and Teresh attempted a palace coup. But he reported them and saved the king and the entire nation. Both people saw challenges that had the tendency of being left alone, and more so as they felt secured; but they also knew that the price of doing nothing could be far more devastating. They were motivated by the possibility, not the guarantee, that they were positioned to fulfill destiny in "such a time as this" (Esther 4:15). Esther was willing to face the risk, declaring: "I will go...and if I perish, I perish!" (Esther 4:16).

Esther and Mordecai exercised great courage that had the potential of undermining their positions, which in the case of Mordecai was his enviable post as the kingdom's chief security officer, and for Esther the highly esteemed position as queen. They did not let their secured positions stand in the way of fulfilling their destinies. Esther's courage to save her people as part of her destiny landed her a spot in the Holy Bible.

Let's try a quick quiz. Without referring to your Bible at this time, what was the name of the Persian king to whom Esther was wife and queen? Answer is_____.

Most people would not get the answer without looking it up. The reason is because no one really cares about *Ahasuerus* today. He was very possibly the most popular and powerful king of his time – in the Persian kingdom and perhaps the world. Ahasuerus ruled over more than 127 provinces from India to Ethiopia (Esther 1:1) and is yet irrelevant today compared to Esther, who overcame fear and discouragement, did not make excuses when it came time to take appropriate action, and refused to be complacent in order to fulfill her individual destiny as well as Israel's corporate destiny. When we fulfill our destinies, our stories outlive us. Esther's story, like those of many others, outlives her.

We will be reminded of many who have made their marks in the sands of time as they overcame fears, discouragements, excuses, and complacency. They faced paralyzing uncertainties and frightful barriers and oppositions. But they would not yield to negative crowd pressures. They stepped away from the status quo. They made choices that brought them into prominence and helped to advance the fulfillment of their destinies. Though caught amidst the blinding floodlights of destiny busters like us, they did not stand still in self-pity or retreat in fear. They refused the easy path of least resistance.

What they did then still works today. The destiny busters they conquered then can be conquered today, if you resolve to. You must *be strong and courageous* as God told Joshua (Joshua 1:6, 9, 18). You must muster strength and courage to overcome the challenges life presents you. You must look past your fears and discouragements and go in faith and boldness to walk the path of your destiny. When you are at intersections and crossroads of life and are faced with uncertainties and hurdles, you need to move on ahead. Those are the times you need to activate your "can do" attitude in order to ensure your altitude. Retreating from challenges and resorting to what appears as humanly safe and comfortable shouldn't be entertained. Take the fight to the enemy's doorsteps if need be. Just do not surrender. Surrendering could leave you immobile and incapacitated like the deer. Do not abort your destiny.

Below is a table that explores common destiny busters and ways to overcome them. First, let's complete the following exercise.

Chapter Exercise:
1. Write down major initiatives you would like to accomplish in the next five years. Don't worry about fears and discouragements (resources, challenges, handicaps, etc.).

Describe where you would like to be in five years?

2. Write down everything you consider as destiny busters, challenges, or deterrents to your ability to accomplish your initiatives.

3. Now write down action plans that will help you overcome those concerns, fears, discouraging factors, etc. I recommend that you speak with those who have already done what you are planning to do. Find out how they scaled the hurdles and overcame the challenges in areas where your initiatives are similar to their accomplishments. Ponder and pray about challenges that may be unique to you as an individual.

4. Write down the rewards/benefits that could result from accomplishing the initiatives you set out to do. Highlight or put those in bold print.

	Goals & Initiatives	Challenges	Action plans	Rewards & Benefits
1.				
2.				
3				
4				

Table of Destiny Busters (Descriptions and Remedies):

Destiny Busters	Description	Remedy
Fear	• Feelings and thoughts of inadequacy • Thoughts of failing	• Build your faith through the Word of God. • Refrain from anything that feeds fear, including negative media and people
Bad association	• Keeping company with the wrong crowd (see Psalm 1)	• Examine and weed out bad influences from your life. • Resolve to be different if that remains the only option.
Bad habits	• Behavioral patterns that are detrimental to you and others	• Identify those patterns and stop. • Be accountable. • Get help from credible sources.
Discouragement	• Listening to negative words • Responding to past unsuccessful attempts • Taking cues from those that have failed • Uncertainty	• Be strong and courageous (see Joshua 1:6-9). • Encourage yourself as David did. • Listen to God. • Reflect on the benefits that will come with accomplishing your goals. The benefits might be worth the momentary sacrifice.
Procrastination	• Waiting for perfect conditions	• Take action without delay (See Ecclesiastes 11:4). • Be accountable to someone who can help motivate you.

Complacency	• Being content at the present spot when there is more • Mindset that things will work out at the appropriate time	• Identify your dreams and share them with others with positive attitudes, especially those who have already accomplished in similar endeavors. • Confide in Prompters, Enablers, Supporters, and Preservers (see chapter 6).
Excuses	• Reasons why something cannot be done • Reasons why timing is not right	• Identify the benefits of stepping out in faith. • Get a good mentor. • Listen to the Word of God. • Get up and confront what seems challenging.
Ignorance	• Lack of knowledge • State of being oblivious	• Acquire knowledge. • Present a teachable spirit at all time. Be ready to learn from others.
Negative confessions	• Permitting others to speak negatively into your life • Receiving negative counsel • Speaking negatively about your life.	• Look for scriptures that deal with your situation. See how the Bible heroes of faith overcame and be ready to do the same. • Declare positive things over your life (remember, life and death are in the power of your tongue).

Chapter Thirteen:

Staying On Course

"For in Him we live and move and have our being, as also some of your own poets have said, 'for we are also His offspring.'"
- Acts 17:28

"Every man has his own destiny; the only imperative is to follow it, to accept it, no matter where it leads him."
– Henry Miller

Life's journey can be likened to embarking on a major road trip. You prepare as much as you can and then set off with a destination in mind. It is impossible to anticipate in detail every event that will occur on the way and to plan ahead of time accordingly. You embark on the journey with a broad view and the *hope* that all will go as planned. As you travel, it is inevitable that you will run into a number of unforeseen circumstances—heavy traffic, accidents, inclement weather conditions, defective equipment, and so forth—that could unduly delay your trip or stop it altogether. You may come to roadblocks that require you to *detour* from your original route. When that happens, you need clear road signs to reconnect you back on the right track to your destination. That is how it is with the journey of life.

God created everyone with a purpose and destination. He determines the appropriate starting point for our life's journey and puts signposts along the way to help us discern whether or not we are on the right path. Circumstances of life attempt every so often to derail us from the path to our destiny. Many have taken detours in life, and where they are not sufficiently discerning, they have lost sight of their destiny. They gave up easily when they considered that they just could not figure it out. Others may have attempted to get back on track but were looking in the wrong direction. They got caught up in a vain search for wealth, money, prestige, popularity, and fame. Others consulted with mediums, astrologers, and other unholy spiritual avenues in their bid for directions but have further enslaved themselves under spurious spiritual covers and ended up misplaced and unfulfilled.

Originating Reference Point

The primary reason we are kept on life's right path toward our destiny is the hope we have of reaching a predetermined destination. Against all odds, we are inclined to forge ahead toward that destination, irrespective of daunting distractions. We have made up our minds that we will follow the journey's road signs and stay on course.

When people do not know where they are going, hopelessness makes its appeal. It begins to manifest itself when people listen to conflicting voices suggesting what their destiny ought to be. In such cases, it becomes easy to have a situation where someone's initial destination changes to what friends and societal values point to. While the different promptings may be done with good intentions, it is often necessary to stop and rethink whether or not you are on the right track, especially if it runs at odds with the paths to initial destination that you set out on. If you become uneasy in your spirit about the overall direction of your life, it may indicate that you need to get back to the Originating Reference Point – God.

God said to Jeremiah: "I knew you before I formed you in your mother's womb. Before you were born I set you apart and appointed you as my prophet to the nations" (Jeremiah 1:5). What God said about Jeremiah is very much true about each of us. He foreknew us and created us for specific purpose. "For we are God's handiwork, created in Christ Jesus to do good works, which God prepared in advance for us to do" (Ephesians 2:10). Any journey to a destination outside of God's plan will inevitably end in hopelessness. We find our true path when we allow God to guide us "for in Him we live and move and have our being, as also some of your own poets have said, 'for we are also His offspring'" (Acts 17:28).

God does not only give us answers to the questions we ask, He also endows us with the qualities and capabilities to decide rightly when in doubt. As distinct from animals, we can, together with God, find the way to successfully fulfill our destiny as we ask Him for revelation (Deuteronomy 29:29). After all, we are reminded in Malachi 3:1-18 that God is the great King of the entire universe and we are "fearfully and wonderfully" made in His image and likeness (Psalm 139:14, Genesis 1:26-27). When our Father chooses to conceal a matter, we have the right as His dear children to search it out. "It is the glory of God to conceal a matter, but the glory of kings is to search out a matter" (Proverbs 25:2). God gives us the ability to discover answers to the questions of life, including those questions pertaining to destiny. He drops clues and signs along the way, and if we would be careful enough to discern what He is saying we would find answers in our past and present happenings.

We have limited knowledge and understanding of our destinies and how to bring about fulfillment. Only God knows all things and gives us those needed road signs along life's journey. Without proper understanding of the signs along the way, we become susceptible to making major mistakes, living in frustration and perhaps missing our destination altogether. We need to read the signs along the way and stay with the last sign we received from God until we receive further directions.

Humans are prone to labeling where there is insufficient understanding of behavioral patterns. Labeling or make-beliefs should never replace clues, which come most often naturally. By boxing your child into the disability case of ADHD (attention deficit hyperactive disorder), for example, may prove harmful to the fulfillment of his destiny. Rather than labeling, ADHD traits may be observed quite all right but with the desire to get a cure and to help the child fulfill his destiny notwithstanding. Walt Disney, Isaac Newton, Pablo Picasso, John F. Kennedy, Michael Jordan, Winston Churchill, Vincent Van Gogh, and Albert Einstein are among those believed to have had ADD (attention deficit disorder).These people excelled in different disciplines including entertainment, sciences, government, arts, etc. Walt Disney is said to have had early interests in arts.

God's thoughts and ways differ from ours. God's methods are far superior to ours, so we should seek to see from His vantage point and follow His directions. Everyone that follows God's leading always succeeds and finds fulfillment. The Bible is clear that: "The steps of a good man are ordered by the LORD, and He delights in his way" (Psalm 37:23). In Romans 8:29, we find that God foreknew and predestined us. God holds the key to our destiny. For everyone that loves God, the issue of what we are to be and how shouldn't be a struggle because God has it all figured out and covered in advance. The family we are born into and our past experiences aren't barriers to the fulfillment of our destinies. God uses lowly origin and bad life experiences to accomplish His plans and purposes just as He does backgrounds of royalty and impeccable pasts.

What's more, events of our lives that are taken for granted could very well be permitted to help us stay on course, or help our mid-course corrections. We could avoid premature exits and abandonment of destiny if we would stay the course and pay close attention to our inner promptings. However, should we get off course for any reason we need to look out for directions so that we can be reconnected back to the right paths. The beauty of our God is that He affords us more than one opportunity – if we turn to Him.

Joseph's life was filled with clues that pointed to his destiny. Born as the eighth child into Jacob's family, his was a case of progeny that defied birthing order. What mattered in his case was whether or not he would make right choices and stay on course, with the barrage of trials that confronted him along the way. In Genesis 37:7-9 we are told that Joseph had *dreams* that provided insight into his destiny. He was convinced that the dreams were divinely inspired, and he therefore would not give up on them by careless living. Divine insights and revelations either from dreams or visions will go a long way to keeping us on course. Wisdom from God on the proper interpretation of dreams/visions is helpful in order to stay on course to destiny.

In the Dungeon

Joseph had several setbacks that would have provided "good" excuses for derailment. He was thrown into the cistern by his brothers with the intent of killing him (Genesis 37:20), but he was supernaturally saved. He was made an object of merchandise, but God redeemed him. He was falsely accused of infidelity in a home where he had proven faithful, but God used every dilemma to advance his destiny. In it all, Joseph behaved wisely. These unfavorable events did not determine Joseph's ultimate outcome. Rather, God caused the events and their timing to work in his favor, in furtherance of his destiny. To rehearse Romans 8:28, Joseph was walking in the light of "we know that in all things God works for the good of those who love him, who have been called according to His purpose."

God made everything work for the furtherance of Joseph's destiny as long as he stayed on course, not compromising his faith or seeking shortcuts on the pathways to his destiny. And because he stayed the course, he consistently rose to the top in every situation and circumstance that confronted him.

Our dreams, passions, past experiences, prophecies made over us, inhibitions, interests, and desires all hold vital clues to our destinies. I cannot emphasize enough the importance of paying close attention to them as clues toward fulfilling your destiny. For those clues to develop to fulfillment, we need to stay on course, especially in critical times when there are contrary suggestions about what we should pursue or which way to go.

David's Path

David's life is yet another model from which we can learn important lessons on staying the course. Though he was the youngest in his family and was not so popular among his brethren, he would not let the challenges of life hinder the advancement of his destiny. In the end it was David who, from among his taller, more impressive brothers, would be anointed king of Israel (1 Samuel 16:1-13).

A little later, David heard of Goliath's threats when he went to visit his brothers at the bidding of his father. He saw all the men of Israel tremble at the sight of Goliath (1 Samuel 17:23-25). David's passion was aroused, and instead of being fearful and fleeing he was ready to confront Goliath. His calling and anointing pulled him to encounter Goliath and made it possible for him to prevail. The defeat of the Philistine was an astounding clue to what God would continue to accomplish for Israel through David. His faithful determination to stay on course when he encountered a lion and a bear while tending his father's sheep was sufficient reason for God to see him as a man after His heart, who would fulfill His plan and purpose. In 1 Samuel

17:31 David's passion and interests made way for him because he pursued them. Where many ran for fear, he stood with courage. He discerned an opportunity to take away Israel's shame and to restore God's glory.

For David, each encounter, whether with the predators (the lion and the bear) or with Goliath, was a steppingstone and motivation to the next phase of his destiny. He trusted the help of God to prevail against extraordinary odds. His anointing by Samuel (before the Goliath encounter) was a witness of God's favor, moving him from insignificance to significance and toward the fulfillment of his preordained destiny. David was not only fired up in his passion against the Philistine, he was also very clear about the reward for ending the reproach against Israel. Obviously being passionate about your dream and sharing it with trusted and wise people will always help you to stay committed to it.

Be accountable

At seventeen, in Nigeria, I had a dream in which I was attending university in the United States with people from diverse backgrounds. I believed passionately that the dream was a revelation from God to inform me of the next phase in my life and held onto it. I knew the dream would ultimately come to pass. It was not long afterwards, at eighteen, that God opened the door for me to come to the United States. As I made preparations for the trip, one of my elder sisters asked me an important question: "What do you plan to do upon getting to the United States?" My response was without ambiguity, because I had dreamed I was going to further my education in the U.S.

A few months after, in Boston, I started working with a local union, delivering beer for thrice the minimum wage. I was surrounded by people who thought being a union worker and receiving compensation well above the minimum wage was a privilege to be content with. They did not see why I should aspire to go to the university. After a few months I became complacent and did not pursue my college dream as vigorously as I should have, until my elder sister called and held me accountable. With her encouragement, though I was earning what then appeared to be decent pay for a laborer, I refused to lose sight of the fact that I had a dream to further my education in the United States. It was not long afterward that I gained admission into college and shortly after completed that phase of my journey to destiny.

It helps to discuss your dreams, intentions, and passions with the right people. People that are interested in your success and have the right perspectives about the things you aim to accomplish. People that will be pleased to hear you without being jealous, judgmental, or condescending. People that can hold you accountable and keep you focused on the right path – as my sister did.

Signs along the paths to destiny are multifaceted. They might also turn out to be incremental. Issues of life might confront from many angles. They may range from "easy to conquer" to "difficult to confront." You cannot tell with any degree of certainty the source or magnitude of life's challenges. Life's challenges, as signs, will be there to point you further along to fulfill your destiny and arrive at your ultimate destination.

Chapter questions:

1. Have you been derailed from the pathways to your destiny? Retrace your steps and get back on course.

2. Do you have abandoned aspirations that you need to pick back up again? Do it.

3. What is your current phase in your journey? What about the next phase? If unsure, prayerfully ask God where you should be one year, and five years from now. Begin to work toward it.

4. Is there someone to whom you can be accountable? Share your goals and aspirations with them and ask them to hold you accountable.

CPSIA information can be obtained at www.ICGtesting.com
Printed in the USA
LVOW121415250213

321445LV00001B/1/P